WHY CULTURE MATTERS MOST

WHY CULTURE MATTERS MOST

DAVID C. ROSE

OXFORD
UNIVERSITY PRESS

OXFORD
UNIVERSITY PRESS

Oxford University Press is a department of the University of Oxford. It furthers
the University's objective of excellence in research, scholarship, and education
by publishing worldwide. Oxford is a registered trade mark of Oxford University
Press in the UK and certain other countries.

Published in the United States of America by Oxford University Press
198 Madison Avenue, New York, NY 10016, United States of America.

© Oxford University Press 2019

Library of Congress Cataloging-in-Publication Data
Names: Rose, David C. (David Charles), author
Title: Why culture matters most / David C. Rose
Description: New York, NY : Oxford University Press, [2019] |
Includes bibliographical references and index.
Identifiers: LCCN 2018015163 (print) | LCCN 2018015998 (ebook) |
ISBN 9780199330737 (UPDF) | ISBN 9780199330744 (EPUB) |
ISBN 9780199330720 (hardcover : alk. paper)
Subjects: LCSH: Culture—Economic aspects. | Social systems—Growth. |
Cooperation. | Economic development Classification: LCC HM621 (ebook) |
LCC HM621 .R6725 2018 (print) |DDC 306—dc23
LC record available at https://lccn.loc.gov/2018015163

CONTENTS

Preface

A few countries are wonderful places to live, work, and raise a family. A few are dreadful. Most are somewhere in between. There is little disagreement about which countries belong in each category. And if you ask why these countries are so different, most people will answer that it has much to do with differences in culture.

The theories people offer for why culture is so important range from banal to bizarre, from innocuous to disturbing. But their powers of observation are in good working order. Evidence of the importance of culture is all around us. Culture in the form of moral beliefs—the focus of this book—affects nearly everything people do and the kind of societies they build.

Many continue to resist cultural explanations for the differential success of societies. This is probably because if culture matters most, then successful societies need more than strong institutions, wise policies, and good leaders—all of which are things more easily changed than culture. This appears to rob us of hope for improving the quality of life of those living in impoverished societies or living in impoverished communities within rich societies.

But increasingly intellectuals, researchers, and scholars have been rediscovering the importance of culture. Consider the influence of Lawrence Harrison and Samuel Huntington's edited collection *Culture Matters*, Deirdre McCloskey's trilogy on the role virtues played in the rise of capitalism, Steven Covey's *The Speed of Trust*, and David Brooks's *The Social Animal, The Road to Character*, as well as many of his columns in the *New York Times*.

Over the last three decades there has been an explosion of academic research on culture. Nearly everyone now agrees that culture is simply too important to ignore even if discussing it is often uncomfortable. But there is, as yet, no general theory of culture that connects it to societal success. So this book presents neither a history of cultural evolution nor a review of statistical evidence to build a case for the importance of culture. Abundant historical and empirical research has already made that case.

This book explains *why* culture matters by proposing a new theory of *how* it can work to make the good life possible for nearly everyone. Unlike anything else, culture channels how we employ our capacity for rational thinking. Rationality helps us make sense of the world and make good decisions. But within any group it can also help us figure out how to promote our welfare at the expense of the common good. And, across groups, it can help *us* figure out how to benefit at the expense of *them*, thereby stoking our penchant for tribalism.

We have known about this problem for a long time. It is the subject of countless campfire tales, fables, plays, novels, movies, and religious texts. Some cultures get around it by crowding out opportunism with beliefs and practices that severely suppress rational thinking generally. In so doing, many produce poor societies that support little individual freedom. But in a few places in the world, culture suppresses opportunism, not rationality, through moral beliefs that make opportunism irrational. This produces trust by channeling rather than suppressing rationality and thereby produces societies in which general prosperity and freedom are the norm.

Trust is the key to the good life. Virtually everything good about any society depends on trust or is strengthened by trust. High-trust societies are the key to unlocking the unfathomable power of cooperation. They promote general prosperity through trust-dependent free market institutions, and they promote freedom through trust-dependent democratic institutions. This book explains why such highly desirable *free market democracies* are inherently unstable unless a critical mass of social trust is sustained. It also explains why free market democracies, which have done so much good in the world, are prone to undermining the very trust that makes them possible.

This book argues that culture is the key to having a high-trust society. Culture works by directing the ends to which individual rationality is employed. Whether culture does this in a way that promotes general prosperity and freedom by creating and sustaining a high-trust society depends mostly on the kind of moral beliefs that are culturally transmitted.

Culturally transmitting *trust-producing moral beliefs* is necessary for building a high-trust society, but it is not sufficient. Such beliefs must also be transmitted in great measure, but unfortunately the deck is stacked against this happening in sufficient measure even in ideal circumstances. Most societies do not address this problem well, which is why most societies are not high-trust societies, so the power of cooperation is largely bottled up in small-group contexts.

Humans dominate all other species. Our capacity for culture and the culture-gene evolutionary process it unleashed is a big reason why. But this book is not about the story of how culture made us human. That fascinating story is already well laid out by the pioneering work of Christopher Boehm, Samuel Bowles, Robert Boyd, Herbert Gintis, Natalie Henrich, Joseph Henrich, Peter Richerson, and others. This book attempts to explain why culture, more than anything else, explains the differential success of the societies that humans went on to build.

David C. Rose
28 February 2018

Acknowledgments

I thank the HFL Foundation, the Earhart Foundation, the Templeton Foundation, and the Office of International Studies & Programs at the University of Missouri–St. Louis for research support. Henry F. Langenberg and John Prentis entrusted me with the Discussion Club for many years and that opened many doors for me. The late Jack Repcheck was a mentor and dear friend, and his enthusiasm for this book meant the world to me.

As important as Milton Friedman was to my first book, Douglass North was to this one. Harold Demsetz, Deirdre McCloskey, and Oliver Williamson helped me by calling attention to mistakes in my thinking. Robert Frank's pioneering work provided the intellectual foundation for much of this book. In our time together in the Galapagos Islands, Robert Boyd made me completely rethink the concept of culture and Robin Dunbar convinced me that group size was the big story. That trip celebrated Charles Darwin's birthday and I will be forever grateful to Deepak Lal for inviting me to speak at such an important event. I also received encouragement or input from Pete Boettke, Bruce Caldwell, David Colander, Jonathan Haidt, James Otteson, Robert Putnam, Hilton Root, and David Sloan Wilson.

As important as all of these people were, the truth is that my sons, Chris and Matt, and especially my wife, Angela, gave me the most help in sorting things out in my mind. Finally, being the spouse of a writer is notoriously bad, but being the spouse of an economist has to be worse. My wife had to endure both, but she never wavered in her support of me or of my work. That support made all the difference.

Prologue

When Lloyd broke into the open, he cursed. Even in the low light of early dawn it was obvious that others had not stuck to the agreement to limit grazing to 10 cows. The village common couldn't take more grazing than that, and everyone knew it.

Yet again he muttered to himself: *Why can't people be trusted to stick to the agreement? Anyone can see what's going to happen!*

What was happening to the common was maddening. Everyone knew overgrazing was a road to ruin. Yet the worse the common became, the more people overgrazed it.

Everyone also agreed to keep up the common by clearing brush. But even Lloyd was now tempted to break both agreements, for what was the point of trying to save the common when ruin was assured no matter what he did? He might as well feed his cows well while he still could and stop wasting his time clearing brush from a common that was destined to return to forest.

The villagers were caught up in a foolish outcome, but they were not fools. They had meetings. They made rules. Nothing worked. What drove them was not foolishness but a refusal to be played as fools by others. And, incredibly, their behavior was completely rational. The village and its common was so large that villagers correctly surmised that if they grazed an extra cow or skipped a day clearing brush, it would change nothing.

If the village were small, the harm done to the community by any farmer breaking either agreement would be substantial, so most farmers would feel too guilty to cheat even if they knew they could get away with it. But small, isolated villages are destined to be poor villages. Might there be a way to get those who live in a very large village to be as trustworthy as those who live in a small village? The answer is yes—through culture.

WHY CULTURE
MATTERS MOST

1

Introduction

What explains the differential success of societies? This is one of our oldest and most important questions. The society one lives in powerfully affects one's quality of life no matter how talented one is and no matter how hard one tries. If we want people to have good lives, the first step is to have successful societies for them to live in.

Economic historian David S. Landes (2000) famously quipped, "If we learn anything from the history of economic development, it is that culture makes almost all the difference."

This book proposes a new theory to explain why it is indeed culture—not genes, geography, institutions, policies, or leadership—that ultimately determines the differential success of societies. The theory explains why culture is the key to understanding why most societies never become highly successful and why so many highly successful societies eventually falter.

The phrase "successful society" means different things to different people. But few would argue that a society that produces widespread material deprivation or denies most people freedom is a successful society. It may be a society that successfully enriches a tyrant and his supporters, but that is hardly a successful *society*. This suggests that, all else the same, the greater the proportion of citizens who are both prosperous and free, the more successful a society is.[1]

So why do some societies enjoy a condition of general prosperity while most, throughout human history, do not? The short answer is that some are able to unleash much of the awesome power of cooperation but most are not. And why do some societies enjoy high levels of freedom while most, throughout human history, do not? The short answer is that some are able to efficaciously employ democracy to serve as a check on government power but most are not.

Achieving general prosperity and freedom is the key to the good life, to best supporting essentially what Nobel Prize–winning economist Edmund Phelps calls *mass flourishing*.[2] This requires having a society that can be well described as a thriving *free market democracy*. Since many of the institutions that support free market economies and democratic government are trust dependent, the key to having a thriving free market democracy is having a high-trust society.

My central claim is that culture is the key to creating the high-trust societies that best support free market democracy and therefore best produce sustainable mass flourishing. So the most successful societies are not necessarily the ones with the smartest or the best-educated people, or the ones with the most natural resources. Too many poorly performing societies are filled with very smart and well-educated people and are located in the midst of ample natural resources. The most successful societies are those whose cultures can sustain a high-trust society.

Certain kinds of moral beliefs about right and wrong are crucial for producing trustworthy individuals. Just wanting to be moral is not enough. When such beliefs are taught to children at a very young age, they instantiate moral tastes that solve a deep problem associated with rational decision-making. This problem normally makes it impossible to presume that strangers in a large and diverse society can be trusted in most circumstances. Culture can therefore be said to matter as content, because moral beliefs that produce highly trustworthy individuals—the substrate of any high-trust society—are obviously part of that society's culture.

But culture also matters instrumentally. This is because the cultural transmission of ideas differs significantly from other forms of transmission. Culture transmits moral beliefs in a way that makes commitment to them so credible and widespread that individuals can automatically depend upon nearly everyone else abiding by them. In a high-trust society this results in being able to presume nearly everyone else will be trustworthy in nearly every circumstance, even in large-group contexts involving diverse peoples. The phrase *trust-producing culture* will therefore refer to the sufficiently strong cultural transmission of *trust-producing moral beliefs*.

In this book I adopt a broad definition of culture that comports with the anthropological sense of the word. *Culture pertains to knowledge transmitted across generations through imitation and teaching rather than through genes.* Culture must therefore be taught and learned generation after generation. This makes culture flexible and therefore far more adaptable than genes. But this also makes culture fragile and therefore a foolish thing to take for granted.

What makes beliefs and practices *cultural* beliefs and practices? Beliefs and practices that are consistently held and followed within societies but that vary widely across societies are precisely what most people have in mind when they use the word "culture." This means culture is not sharply defined but is, instead, a matter of degree, which may explain why culture has proven so difficult to build into formal theoretical models of political economy.

For most people, culture first brings to mind differences in practices. Cultural practices can differ dramatically from society to society. Many of these differences are most evident when comparing small societies to one another (e.g., Inuit versus Bedouin). But this book is not about differences in cultural practices or small societies. This book is about how differences in moral beliefs affect the way large societies function.

Prevailing moral beliefs are the key to overcoming a fundamental impediment to humans cooperating in very large-group contexts. That impediment is the tendency for individual rationality to undermine the common good. This is a very well-known problem. It is a central issue in the study of political economy going back at least to Plato. It is a critical element of the individual- versus group-selection debate in the theory of evolution.[3] It is a subject of great concern to all of the social sciences and has been studied extensively by game theorists.[4]

One way that individual rationality can undermine the common good is that individuals rationally decide to behave in untrustworthy ways. In large-group contexts in particular, dishonesty often pays off handsomely while causing imperceptible harm because harm is often spread over so many people that no other individual can even notice. As a result, little if any guilt is aroused by innate moral intuitions that make us reluctant to harm other persons.[5] The problem is that when many behave dishonestly, we cannot trust each other as a rule of thumb and the harm to society from not being able to do so is substantial.

This book explains how culture can get around this problem better than anything else. Trust-producing culture can produce a high-trust society that supports free market democracy, which is the key to mass flourishing. Societies that best support mass flourishing tend to be the most successful as long as they don't destroy themselves from within. They also tend to be good neighbors because their success does not require preying upon other societies. Trust-producing culture therefore also tends to support international harmony.

The main argument can be summarized in the following list of claims.

1. Mass flourishing is impossible without large-group cooperation. The most successful societies are those that support the greatest scale and scope of cooperation. To get the most out of large-group cooperation we have to be able to trust each other in large-group contexts.

2. Trust comes naturally in small groups because we evolved in small groups. Our genes offer comparatively little help in producing large-group trust. But when trust-producing moral beliefs are culturally transmitted in sufficient measure, a high-trust society can emerge.

3. The set of trust-producing moral beliefs constitutes a *cultural commons*. As is often the case with common ownership, individual rationality tends to work against the common good. In this case unbridled individual rationality works against the high-trust society.

4. Economic development is like climbing a ladder. Each rung corresponds to a larger set of transactions through which the gains from cooperation can be derived. Higher trust lets society climb up the ladder by making ever more trust-dependent transactions viable.

5. The deck is stacked against a society investing enough in trust-producing moral beliefs to best promote the common good. This problem worsens as societies climb the ladder of development. This is why free market democracies are so difficult to create and sustain.

6. Many free market and democratic institutions are highly trust dependent. If trust-producing culture erodes, then general prosperity will fall and democracy will increasingly devolve into a spoils system that stokes political tribalism that can destroy society from within.

How Culture Shaped Us

For well over 100,000 years our species did not dominate the planet, but we now do. Why? Pathbreaking books such as Robert Boyd and Peter Richerson's *Culture and the Evolutionary Process* (1985), Peter Richerson and Boyd's *Not by Genes Alone* (2005), Natalie and Joseph Henrich's *Why Humans Cooperate* (2007), and Samuel Bowles and Herbert Gintis's *A Cooperative Species* (2011) strongly suggest that it was not simply because our genes made us ever smarter.[6]

The basic argument is that different parts of the world presented us with different challenges. Culture made it possible to adapt to these different challenges much faster than genes could. But when our behavior changes to cope with a specific environment, genes that support such behavior are reinforced in the population over time. This produces not just behavioral adaptation to local conditions but also genetic adaptation as well. It is becoming increasingly clear that culture is not just a product of, but is also a writer of, the human genetic recipe.[7]

As humans started to enjoy greater success relative to all other species, a number of evolutionary feedback processes began to unfold. The more humans dominated all other species, the truer it became that competition with other humans affected survival more than competition with other species. This likely contributed to an intraspecies cognitive arms race that explains why our intelligence is so far beyond all other existing species today.

But as important as our intelligence is to our success, it is unlikely that our superior intelligence is the sole explanation for our ability to dominate other species. Joseph Henrich's *The Secret of Our Success* (2016) presents a compelling argument for why our superior individual intelligence has less to do with our species success than our "collective brain." In short, we are qualitatively different from other highly cooperative species because our capacity for culture allows us to socially connect on grand scales and accumulate knowledge over generations. Our individual intelligence advantage over other species therefore pales in comparison to the advantage afforded by our collective brain made possible by culture. But stretching the size of the groups within which we can cooperate was no small feat. Robin Dunbar's famous number (~150 individuals) for the largest group size within which we naturally live and cooperate well is very small indeed.[8]

It is now becoming clear that even before humans dominated all other species, competition with each other also contributed to a cultural arms race. This new margin of competition involved developing and reinforcing traits to support ever more effective cooperation in ever larger groups over ever longer periods. This, in turn, led to the selection for genes that enabled us to benefit even more from cultural beliefs and practices that supported cooperation in contexts that were beyond the reach of our small-group genes.

Culture therefore became an ever more important determinant of group success, which led to culture's importance feeding on itself. This led those groups whose genes favored traits that supported the rapid and flexible cultural transmission of beliefs and practices to prevail over those that did not. Ideas can be discovered, taught, and learned much faster than genes can adapt.[9]

So because of faster adaptation, memes—tiny bits of culture— became ever more important relative to genes in explaining the differential success of groups. Increasingly it was culture, and institutions made possible by culture, that determined which groups dominated the others. In short, culturally transmitted beliefs and practices helped us transcend our small-group limitations to cooperate ever more effectively in ever larger groups.

The rise of agriculture allowed humans to build large societies. Competition between large societies induced further changes in culture and institutions. The societies that were the winners in this competition were, by definition, the most successful societies. But that does not mean they were the best societies to live in or that would do the best job advancing the species generally. Few today would choose to live in ancient Sparta over ancient Athens, and few would argue that Sparta's effect on the rise of Western civilization equaled that of Athens.[10]

Culture can also transmit moral beliefs that legitimize the subjugation of other individuals, treating them as mere means to ends and thereby showing little respect for them as individual persons. For a long time societal success normally benefited a minority elite at the expense of misery endured by the vast majority of people. For many people in many societies for much of history, this life was likely worse than the hunter-gatherer existence of their ancestors.[11]

Culture and Religion

Beliefs about right and wrong are often related to religion, but moral beliefs and religion are not equivalent. Many of the same moral beliefs about right and wrong are prominent in a number of religions, but some moral beliefs only appear in one or a few religions. Moreover, religions are more than a set of moral beliefs about right and wrong. Religions also have rules for behavior involving various practices, rites, and rituals, that are clearly nonmoral in nature.

Moral beliefs about right and wrong are also more than a list of endorsed moral values. Two religions may share a similar historical narrative and set of moral values yet differ substantially in how these values are logically related to one another. This can produce very different conclusions about morally proper behavior. In chapter 3 I discuss how one such difference is the key to producing trustworthy individuals.

Some modern researchers are trying to explain the ubiquity of belief in a God or gods by improving our understanding of the role that a belief in a God or gods might play in the evolution of societies. In the last decade or so there has been an increasing emphasis on the critical role played by moral behavior in coordinating social behavior. This comports with the shift in religion, from mostly providing a way to explain the world around us to addressing matters of right and wrong, coinciding with the rise of large societies.[12]

But the rise of large societies, even very religious ones, is a long way from the rise of societies that can support mass flourishing. Chapters 3 and 4 explain why mass flourishing requires more than a God who serves as an omnipresent monitor, rewarder, and punisher. This is because many moral beliefs—especially those that come most naturally to us—do not produce reliable trustworthiness even for highly moral people. In some societies people can be very eager to please their God and still not be regarded as trustworthy by others even in their own society. The connection between culture and religion is very deep and I discuss it in much more detail in chapter 8.

Culture and Institutions

In the social sciences the word "institutions" refers to consistent patterns in how we do things. Consistent patterns have the effect of reducing the risk of being cheated by others and therefore reduce the cost of transacting. The rise of formalism in the social sciences through most of the 20th century reduced interest in this approach to the study of institutions. But due in large part to the pioneering work of John Commons and Ronald Coase, the rise of transaction cost analysis provided a new and powerful way to think about institutions.

Coase won the Nobel Prize in Economics mostly for two seminal articles that employed transaction cost analysis in new and powerful ways. The first article, "The Nature of the Firm" (1937), explained the existence of firms as organizational forms that minimize transaction costs relative to market coordination of economic activity. The second article, "The Problem of Social Cost" (1960), demonstrated that the existence of transaction costs obscures the true nature of the problem of externalities.[13]

Douglass North and Oliver Williamson, both also Nobel Prize winners, took the lead in advancing the view that institutions create value for society by reducing transaction costs and thereby maximizing the scale and scope of economic transactions. The work of Armen Alchian, Harold Demsetz, Elinor Ostrom, Hernando de Soto, Avner Greif, and others also helped revive interest in the study of economic institutions by applying modern tools of theoretical and empirical analysis, which came to be known as *new institutional economics*.

It is hard to overstate the importance of institutions. It is also hard to overstate how strongly institutional analysis has affected the study of economic development and economic history. For an example one need look no further than Daron Acemoglu and James Robinson's highly influential book *Why Nations Fail* (2012). Acemoglu and Robinson explain the differential success of societies by arguing that it is the absence of "institutions, institutions, institutions" that broadly explains the existence of poorly performing societies.

Institutional analysis has proven so fruitful that many institutionalists view the study of culture as either superfluous or as properly subsumed into the institutional paradigm. Oliver Williamson won the Nobel Prize in Economics with Elinor Ostrom for his work on institutions and argued that trust—an important concept in the study of culture—was largely a distraction.

Williamson and many other institutional scholars view institutions more as substitutes for than as complements to trust.

In their view, institutions provide what Toshio Yamagishi refers to as "assurance" in the large-group contexts where genuine trust does not exist.[14] So trust is not necessary in a story of how a free market economy works because institutions solve the problems that trust would solve (but cannot solve) in the context of large-scale economic activity. So until recently the study of institutions has had the effect of crowding out or subsuming into second-class status the study of culture, particularly culture as it relates to trust.

A problem with this line of reasoning is that just because something is not necessary does not mean it cannot produce a better outcome. One could argue that guns are unnecessary because spears have already demonstrated they can kill the enemy. But wouldn't this be a foolish argument for why you didn't buy guns at a low price when they became available? Spears might be good enough, but guns are almost certainly better.

Similarly, institutions might get the job done rather well, but for many kinds of transactions trust might get the job done better. To maximize the gains from cooperation, a society must exhaust all potential cooperative gains. Trust lowers transaction costs even further than institutions alone. Whether doing so leads to a net improvement depends on whether the gains from lower transaction costs outweigh the cost of creating and sustaining a high-trust society. This question must be addressed before presuming that trust is superfluous.

Eric Jones, in his book *Cultures Merging: A Historical and Economic Critique of Culture* (2006), argues that the recent resurgence of interest in cultural explanations is largely a mistake. He argues that culture is not as fixed as those who appeal to cultural explanations seem to believe. Instead, culture rapidly evolves in response to changing conditions, including changes to institutions. This is a strong point, but it makes a more compelling case for why culture and institutions are codetermined than it does for the primacy of institutions over culture.

I contend that if one is to be viewed as primary to the other, it is culture that is primary to institutions. This is because the key to the good life is having a thriving free market democracy, but that requires many highly trust-dependent institutions. If only culture can produce a high-trust society, then it follows that trust-dependent institutions follow from culture. The fact that culture clearly adapts to changes in institutions does not invalidate this point; it only means that culture and institutions affect each other.

There is another problem with the "institutions, institutions, institutions" explanation for the differential success of societies. Institutions are basically how we do things. Therefore asserting that they are the key to success is almost tautological since it is hard to imagine a society that does everything like prosperous societies but remains impoverished. Tautological explanations are always correct, but usually unhelpful. It's like being asked, "Why did the building burn down?" and answering, "There was a fire." That's not wrong, but it begs the question of why there was a fire. Similarly, one could be asked, "Why are most people in that society in poverty?" and answering, "It has inadequate institutions." That's also not wrong, but doesn't that raise the question of why its institutions are inadequate?

Finally, institutional scholars have largely figured out which institutions are important and why. There are also plenty of proven templates and plenty of rich countries eager to assist with their implementation. Organizations like the World Bank understand the importance of institutions and are also eager to assist with money and expertise. If insufficient institutions are all there is to explaining the development problem, then all that struggling countries need to do is adopt the required institutions.

The same could be said for adopting the required policies and leaders. We know what good economic policies look like and how good leaders are supposed to act. Many poor countries are democracies. If a struggling country is democratic, why would voters elect bad leaders who, in turn, implement bad policies? If either bad policies or bad leadership is the main problem, then all democracies should be doing well because they possess the ability to get rid of bad leaders who promulgate bad policies.

Some believe that the differential success of societies is largely a matter of corruption. But many institutions exist to thwart corruption. If the country is a democracy, why are these institutions not adopted? If they are adopted but don't work, why don't they work? Why not vote out corrupt leaders? If that is impossible because everyone who runs for office is corrupt, why is this true? The corruption explanation begs more questions than it answers.

Yet another problem with the institutional explanation for the differential success of societies is that in many free market democracies, crucial institutions are unraveling. Many highly successful free market democracies are showing signs of instability. Debt overhang, a run-up in excess reserves in the banking system, social programs that have unfunded liabilities that cannot possibly be met, and the erosion of the rule of law are all instances of institutional failure and are beginning to affect the economic performance and social stability of many countries in the West.

In his book *The Great Degeneration* (2013), Niall Ferguson argues that the shrinking gap between countries in the West and those like China and India has as much to do with the former faltering as it does with the latter rising. Ferguson explains why weakening institutions in the West are the major culprit. So why is it that, over the last half-century, the problem hasn't been an unwillingness by struggling countries to adopt the requisite institutions of a free market democracy so much as it has been an inability to sustain them in societies where they have already produced remarkable success?

The answer to all of these questions is that many of the institutions we take for granted in societies that produce mass flourishing are highly trust dependent. Much as they'd like to, many struggling countries cannot simply adopt these institutions because they have low-trust societies. That is the most important reason why they are struggling in the first place.

A high-trust society can easily adopt trust-dependent institutions if there is reason to do so, but the reverse is not true. Many institutions do not work well in a low-trust society because they are trust dependent, and introducing them does not magically produce a high-trust society. As but one example, consider the rule of law.

Few would argue that the rule of law is not an important institutional foundation for a free market democracy. But the institutional practice of using formal contracts to coordinate business activity, for example, is only as viable as the court system is deemed to be trustworthy. As a general principle, when highly trust-dependent institutions are introduced in low-trust societies, they are quickly abandoned or corrupted. In countries where it is common to bribe judges, for example, the rule of law is largely a mirage.

If trust begins to fall in a high-trust society, institutions that depend upon trust inevitably begin to unravel. So a once-thriving nation cannot simply reset its institutional foundation, because faltering institutions are not the cause of the problem, but a symptom of a deeper problem. That deeper problem is that they are losing their cultural foundation.[15]

In my view, culture and institutions are better viewed as complements than as substitutes.[16] Trust-producing culture is so important precisely because trust-dependent institutions are so important. Institutions that are not trust-dependent are important, too, but they cannot explain why the lowest-trust countries never have the highest-performing economies. We know a great deal about how institutions advanced development. The real work now lies in improving our understanding of how culture and institutions coevolved to produce the most successful societies. Figure 1.1 provides an overview of what I shall argue over the course of this book is the basic relationship between culture, the high-trust society, institutions, and mass flourishing.

Resistance to Cultural Explanations

The idea that culture is an important factor in explaining a society's success is hardly new. Arguments to this effect were made by the ancient Greeks and have been echoed ever since. Anthropologists and sociologists have long recognized the importance of culture. Classical

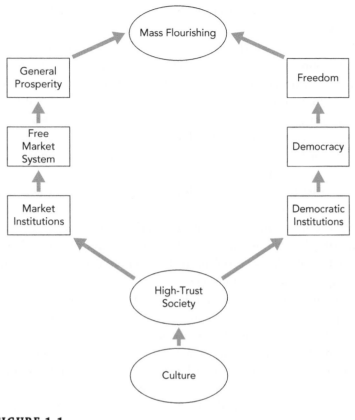

FIGURE 1.1

The relationship between the free market system, democracy, and their respective institutions

economists and the American Founding Fathers appreciated the importance of culture. But with the rise of rational choice theory and neoclassical economics, cultural explanations for social, political, and economic phenomena fell out of favor. Why?

Culture is by nature idiosyncratic, theoretically messy, and empirically difficult to measure. All of this flew in the face of neoclassical economics, which sought the kind of precision and universality that was evident in theoretical physics. This tendency is echoed in modern work that demonstrates the importance of culture through formal modeling. Such work emphasizes the low cost of imitation of cultural practices, and that such imitation produces conformity within societies but is consistent with there being differences in practices across societies.

Moral beliefs don't lend themselves nearly as well to modeling. I suspect that this is part of the reason why the study of moral beliefs has gotten far less traction than the study of cultural practices. Finally, neoclassical economists sought universality in part by avoiding appeals to explanations rooted in tastes, which are normally subjective and therefore hardly universal. To the extent that differences in moral beliefs are viewed as differences in tastes, this likely produced further resistance to cultural explanations.

Another possible reason for resisting cultural explanations is that efforts to improve our understanding of the differential success of societies have been largely rooted in a desire to foster economic development. Cultural explanations are normally viewed as infertile ground for spurring economic development. This is because one can envision changing a society's leaders, policies, laws, and even some of its institutions. But it is much harder, and certainly much more presumptuous, to attempt to change a society's culture.

Finally, after World War II there was a strong negative reaction to eugenic ideas that had become increasingly popular over the course of the 19th century and that were put on horrific display in Nazi Germany. This made discussion of anything that even sounded remotely like eugenics politically incorrect after World War II. Not surprisingly, this made it increasingly fashionable to view the nature-versus-nurture debate as about 10% nature and 90% nurture.

It would seem that the backlash against eugenics should have led to a greater willingness to consider cultural explanations, since there are things genes don't explain well but that culture might. This is part of the appeal of cultural explanations. But many scholars began to treat cultural explanations as one step removed from genetic explanations. Saying that a society's culture might explain a bad outcome was taken as code for the problem being that a given society's people were genetically inferior. This may have been a holdover from the fallacious 19th-century habit of viewing culture as being rather directly derived from genes.

But while the genes we all share give us the capacity for culture, these genes do not transmit cultural beliefs themselves. This is why culture is much more rapidly adaptable than genes. The kinds of moral beliefs that I shall argue are the key to creating high-trust societies therefore have nothing to do genes. These beliefs had to emerge somewhere first, and that was mostly a matter of good luck. It had nothing to do with genes, race, or even the general level of morality.

What's Ahead

This book is divided into two parts. Part I explains how trust-producing culture works in a unique way to promote the common good. Large-group cooperation is shown to be the key to enjoying general prosperity. Large-group trust is then shown to be the key to getting the most out of large-group cooperation. If certain kinds of shared moral beliefs produce a high-trust society and therefore large-group trust, they would be one of that society's most precious assets. But no one owns the set of shared moral beliefs. It is commonly owned by the entire society.

The metaphor of a cultural commons is proposed to embrace this observation about shared moral beliefs. The cultural commons echoes the common pasture made famous in Garrett Hardin's "The Tragedy of the Commons" (1968). In a common pasture, individual rationality undermines the common good through overgrazing of livestock. It is similarly difficult to keep people from abusing the cultural commons and thereby debasing the trust that trust-producing moral beliefs make possible.

The characteristics that moral beliefs must have to produce trustworthy individuals are then discussed. For these moral beliefs to produce a high-trust society, they must be consistently held across members of society. They must also be learned early enough in life to influence decision-making through tastes that are antecedent to rational decision-making.

The rise of mass flourishing is shown to correspond with the rise of the high-trust society, as this allows a society to climb a ladder of development where each rung corresponds to an ever larger set of viable transactions. I show why the deck is rigged against societies investing enough in teaching trust-producing moral beliefs to climb the ladder of development high enough to best promote the common good. The cultural commons is therefore not only subject to abuse, it is also subject to neglect in the form of inadequate investment.

Part II applies this framework to understanding the cultural foundation for free market democracies. Free market democracies require many highly trust-dependent institutions. So just as free market democracies rest on an institutional foundation, that institutional foundation rests on a cultural foundation because culture makes a high-trust society possible.

It is well known that the free market system and democracy have self-reinforcing properties. But trust-dependent institutions require a high-trust society, so if trust falters, many of these institutions will weaken. This can lead to the democratic process becoming a spoils system that stokes political tribalism that destabilizes a society. Such tribalism can induce families to reduce investment in trust-producing moral beliefs. It can also induce families to stress moral beliefs that make it easier to rationalize opportunism. As this process feeds on itself, it can lead to the collapse of once-thriving societies.

I then explore the role the family plays in the transmission of culture and how changing technology has affected this role. I explore how some religions evolved in ways that best put culture to work for producing high-trust societies, and why religious-based terrorism is best understood when we recognize the unique role that culture plays in channeling rationality. I discuss some implications for government and freedom. Finally, I offer an explanation for what is happening to the West and how trust-producing culture that we took for granted for too long might be reinvigorated.

Notes

1. There are individuals, ideological groups, and religious groups who do not believe that society should concern itself with general prosperity or freedom. That such societies persist is a reflection of the awesome power of culture. I will return to this important issue in chapter 4.

2. See Edmund Phelps's (2013) *Mass Flourishing*.

3. See Richard Dawkins's (1976) *The Selfish Gene* or David Sloan Wilson's (2002) *Darwin's Cathedral: Evolution, Religion, and the Nature of Society*.

4. The most famous examples are John Maynard Smith's (1982) *Evolution and the Theory of Games* and Robert Axelrod's (1984) *The Evolution of Cooperation*. But nearly all game theory textbooks cover the commons dilemma, which captures this phenomenon.

5. I use the word *innate* along the lines discussed by Jonathan Haidt (2012) and Gary Marcus (2004), meaning strongly influenced by genes all humans share but better described as prewired than hardwired.

6. Recent work in the academic literature reflects an increasing awareness that culture matters even more than previously thought. See papers Algan and Cahuc (2010), Tabellini (2010), Gorodnichenko and Roland (2011), Luttmer and Singhal (2011), and Lowes et al. (2015).

7. See papers by Richerson et al. (2010) and Gintis (2011) for excellent reviews of the literature pertaining to gene-culture evolution.

8. For a discussion of the factors that impede large-group living and cooperating, see Robin Dunbar's (2016) *Human Evolution* and Coward and Dunbar (2014).

9. Few appreciated culture's role in group selection as well as Nobel Prize–winning economist Friedrich Hayek. He stressed it was not necessary for anyone to understand how traits might increase the chances of survival for individuals or the group, and that many beliefs and practices take the form of traditions whose origins and function are unknown and whose constraint upon human action is often despised (Hayek 1988).

10. I thank Max Gillman for this example.

11. See Jared Diamond's (1987) famous argument to this effect, "The Worst Mistake in the History of the Human Race."

12. See Wade (2015).

13. Externalities are the effects (e.g., toxic smoke from a plant) that some transactions have on the welfare of those who are not direct parties.

14. See Toshio Yamagishi's book, *Trust* (2000).

15. The Nobel Prize–winning economist James M. Buchanan was a strong advocate of using constitutional constraints to deal with such problems. Buchanan, Hayek, and North were among the first economists to view culture and institutions as complements.

16. For an excellent summary of the literature that considers the complementary relationship between culture and institutions see Alesina and Giuliano (2015). See also Gorodnichenko and Roland (2010). See also Bisin and Verdier (2017).

PART I

HOW CULTURE WORKS

2

The Cultural Commons

Cooperating well in small groups is relatively easy because we have had ample time to evolve traits that support small-group trust. We have had comparatively little time to evolve traits that support large-group trust. This is a huge obstacle to economic development because, as we will see shortly, if cooperation is limited to small groups, then general prosperity is impossible. It follows that any part of culture that facilitates large-group trust is an asset to all members of society, a common *cultural* asset.

Cooperation is so important because it involves what game theorists call positive-sum activity. This is the idea that people act together in ways that result in the value of the whole becoming greater than the value of the sum of the parts. In a free market economy most transactions are voluntary, so all parties must believe they will be made better off. But the only way a transaction can make everyone better off is if the value of working together exceeds the value of the sum of what individuals would have produced on their own.[1]

Because the value of the whole is greater than the value of the sum of the parts, cooperation is very different from an activity like dividing a pie—a frequent example of zero-sum activity. Cooperation therefore is more like two people, each able to make one pie, being able to make three instead of two if they work together. Cooperation therefore is the key to having more per person. The more cooperation a society fosters, the more it can flourish, because mass flourishing requires general prosperity, and increasing general prosperity starts with having more per person.

How Cooperation Works

Suppose that working alone you make 10 pies a day and working alone I do too, but working together—cooperating—we make 26. Obviously the whole (26) is greater than the sum of the parts (20). This is therefore a positive-sum activity, and the value of this activity, here 6, is known as the cooperative surplus. It is the expectation of a cooperative surplus that can be divided between us that induces us to cooperate.[2]

There are many reasons for the existence of cooperative surpluses, but the most well known is reaping the gains from specialized production. Think of any activity you might do alone. If someone else joins you to help, it is unlikely he will just copy what you were doing. More likely the two of you will cooperate by dividing the tasks because doing so is the key to more than doubling what you were making alone. This gain from specialized production arises from what Adam Smith called the *division of labor*.

The division of labor can increase productivity so much that it boggles the mind. In his famous example of pin factory production, Adam Smith ([1776] 1981) compared worker productivity for a single pinmaker to worker productivity for 10 pinmakers who divided up the tasks so as to enjoy the gains from specialization. The increase in worker productivity in this real-life example was an incredible 23,900%! Cooperating with each other to enjoy the gains from specialization is therefore no mere detail of economic theory.[3]

Economies of Scale

Adam Smith also pointed out that the larger the group, the more finely tasks can be divided. Suppose there are six separate tasks associated with making pies. With two people the tasks would likely be divided so each person does three. But with six people it is possible to have each person do only one task. Smith argued that in most cases a finer division of labor increases the gains from specialization even more, often *exponentially more*. So specialization is good, but specialization in large rather than small groups is far better.

This was the crux of Smith's argument for free trade in his masterpiece *An Inquiry into the Nature and Causes of the Wealth of Nations*. Foreign trade reduces the list of goods produced in any given country while increasing the demand for the goods that are still produced. This makes it possible for all firms in all countries to become larger so they can more finely divide labor. This increases the amount of goods and services for the same number of people in all countries at the same time.

Maximizing general prosperity requires piling up cooperative surpluses as much as possible. This means engaging in the greatest scale and scope of cooperation possible. Everything else is detail. To say that mass flourishing therefore begins with cooperation is almost tautological.

Opportunism

Most cooperation occurs through transactions, but transacting with others often opens us up to opportunistic victimization. Fear of opportunism drives up the expected cost of transacting with others. If the expected transaction cost exceeds the expected value of the cooperative surplus, such a transaction won't be undertaken voluntarily. Since a society's ability to prosper is derived from its ability to pile up cooperative surpluses, it follows that the more effectively it keeps opportunism from driving up transaction costs, the more it will prosper.

Transaction costs are therefore a formidable impediment to cooperation. As such, they undermine a society's ability to promote the common good. Why can't people figure out how to trust each other so they can solve this problem? The short answer is that individually rational behavior doesn't always produce a socially desirable outcome.

Trust

Recall that Oliver Williamson cautioned economists against focusing on trust as a factor in explaining how free market economies work. In *The Fatal Conceit* (1988), Friedrich Hayek argued that capitalism constituted an extended order of large-group cooperation. Such large-group cooperation was made possible by a legal framework that he viewed as providing a substitute for trust, which he viewed as a small-group phenomenon.

For Hayek and Williamson, many institutions are substitutes for trust in a large society of strangers. For many institutions in many societies, this is certainly true. But that does not mean it has to always be true. Some of the institutions that are crucial for maximizing large-group cooperation are trust dependent. Such institutions obviously cannot serve as a substitute for trust.

Democratic voting is a feature of any thriving free market democracy, but it is clearly a trust-dependent institution. The use of relational contracts is also a feature of any thriving free market democracy because they give firm managers discretion to adapt to changing conditions. But this also gives them greater ability to engage in opportunism. Relational contracts are therefore a trust-dependent institution because decision-makers must be trusted to act on information that only they know in a way that promotes the firm's interest rather than their own.[4]

One thing that dramatically reduces transaction costs is transacting with trustworthy people. If there is a strong social norm of trustworthiness, then it is rational for people to presume others can be trusted in a wide variety of circumstances. The presumptive extension of trust to strangers in most circumstances is an institution that is obviously trust dependent.[5] There are obvious benefits to knowing that virtually all potential transaction partners are trustworthy.

In my view, Hayek, Williamson, and many other social scientists have underestimated the importance of large-group trust. A social norm of trustworthiness is very evident in high-trust societies. It makes highly trust-dependent institutions like democratic voting, relational contracts, and the presumptive extension of trust possible. While Hayek and Williamson are correct to argue that institutions can serve as a substitute for trust in many ways, it is also true that trust is a necessary condition for trust-dependent institutions.

High-trust societies that support both small- and large-group trust through a social norm of trustworthiness are therefore qualitatively different. They are more than low-trust societies that have increased the radius of trust of small-group trust because they make it possible for a society to benefit from having trust-dependent institutions.[6] It is therefore imperative that we understand what creates and sustains large-group trust. Since large-group trust differs significantly across societies, we should not presume it is derived from our basic nature.

Cultural Content

Practices

When someone says the word "culture," for many the image that jumps to mind is some kind of consistent practice within a given society that is unique to that society or, at the very least, is not universal across all societies. Within any given group, cultural practices produce consistency that lowers transaction costs because everyone knows what to expect from others.

Many cultural practices are acquired largely by imitation. Natural selection reinforces the imitation of the most efficient actions. Imitation is valuable because it conserves resources that would otherwise be wasted coming up with the same solutions again and again. Behavior that decreases individual *and* group productivity is not likely to be imitated, at least not for long.[7]

But behavior that benefits the individual at the expense of the group may still be reinforced by natural selection. The smaller the group, the more likely that such behavior will noticeably reduce the welfare of others in the group, which can discourage such behavior.

But the larger the group, the less likely it is that such behavior will noticeably reduce the welfare of anyone in the group.

Because such behavior harms the group as a whole, it is normally done in secret. It may be imitated (children who see their parents break laws are more likely to become lawbreakers) but it will not become a socially endorsed behavior. Behaviors that benefit the group have no reason to be done in secret and will, instead, likely arouse expressions of approval along the lines described by Adam Smith in *The Theory of Moral Sentiments* ([1769] 1982). Moreover, any behavior that contributes to cooperation by catalyzing trust will likely be reinforced even if this was not the original intent of such a practice.

As but one example, if members of a set of groups stumble onto the practice of encouraging intermarriage between groups, this might create family ties that support trust between the groups in that set. This can enable better cooperation between these groups and, in so doing, benefit all of them relative to other sets of groups who do not encourage intermarriage.

Consistency of behavior through cultural practices can also benefit a group by precluding opportunistic behavior. If a given cultural practice leaves little room for opportunism, it is more likely to be replicated than if it opens the door to opportunism. This reduces expected transaction costs and thereby supports greater cooperation.

Beliefs

Douglass North, in his book *Understanding the Process of Economic Change* (2005), explored the role that beliefs played in effectuating adaptive efficiency for societies. He argued this process of adaptation was different from biological adaptation because of the intentionality of the actors involved. North proposed that such decision-making is guided by beliefs.

Cultural practices are more flexible than genes, but it seems rather obvious that in many cases they adapt to change in ways that are only one step removed from genetic adaptation. A slight variation in a practice can be analogous to a genetic mutation. If that variation is more efficient it is likely to be repeated by others, just as a beneficial gene mutation is likely to be replicated in the population. In his book *The Selfish Gene* (1976), Richard Dawkins introduced the concept of memes to convey this concept for both practices and ideas.

But humans also intentionally try to adapt to change. They often know they must adapt in some way to solve a problem. With early humans this happened mostly when confronted with new circumstances arising from the physical environment or rival groups. Today it also happens in response to, among other things, changes in market conditions. But in any case, conscious decision-making that starts at zero each time is very inefficient. Just as reinventing the wheel every time is inefficient, organizing one's thoughts to make decisions from a cognitive blank slate is inefficient. This created an evolutionary return for having beliefs that could provide a framework for efficient decision-making.

Now consider the possibility that a particular set of moral beliefs strongly support a norm of trustworthiness. Precisely what those beliefs might look like will be discussed in the next chapter. By creating a norm of trustworthiness, such trust-producing moral beliefs would directly reduce transaction costs because everyone prefers trustworthy transaction partners. At the same time, such trust-producing moral beliefs would indirectly reduce transaction costs because many institutions that lower transaction costs are themselves highly dependent on trust.

Complex formal contracts, for example, are an important feature of prosperous societies. But such contracts are of little value if the judicial system cannot be trusted. Strong property rights are another important feature of prosperous societies. But property rights are of little value if the government cannot be trusted to fairly enforce them. If the wealth one creates can be easily taken by individuals or by the state, there is no point in exerting effort or investing to create wealth.

Storytelling

The stories people tell in a given society are obviously an important part of its culture. Stories are important because many beliefs are subtler in nature than knowledge about how to accomplish tasks. Beliefs are often abstract, complex, subtle, and therefore difficult to comprehend, especially for children. This may be one reason why humans have evolved such a strong taste for telling and listening to stories, as is evidenced by the incredible amount of time we spend reading novels, going to movies, and watching television.

We have obviously evolved traits that make it easy for us to tell stories and make it possible for stories told by others to hold our attention. Very little of what we know is passed to us through our genes. Storytelling is a means of conveying knowledge that changes too fast to be genetically encoded or that is too subtle or too infrequent to be transferred through the imitation of practices. Consider knowing that one should back away slowly from any poisonous snake. Learning this by imitation is worthless since most people never see a poisonous snake, let alone see someone else back slowly away from one.

Retold stories have a peculiar hold on humans that is especially strong in children. Just think of a small child's desire to be told the same bedtime story over and over or to watch the same video repeatedly. This is indicative of the evolutionary power of culture. We have evolved a preference not just for being told stories but for being told stories repeatedly because a repeated story, if it is not contradicted by experience, is a story more likely to be true.

A story that is repeated a few times but often found to be false is rejected. A story heard once and not contradicted by evidence is not rejected but is still viewed with skepticism since some stories are not true. But a story heard repeatedly and never contradicted by evidence is, with each retelling, believed to be true with ever stronger conviction. So if one hears a story of a particular mammoth hunt that comports with stories of other mammoth hunts, the common elements in all of these stories are likely to be treated as important pieces of information.

Myths play an important role in many cultures. Stories with elements that have been discovered to be false are not likely to be retold (Bob flies over the village in the story, but if we ask Bob to fly he can't). Stories with no elements that have been discovered to be false are more likely to be retold (an invisible god flies over the village). Myths likely evolved because they can be tailored to convey complex and subtle ideas that are difficult to convey through stories rooted in normal life. At the same time, they involve worlds and characters beyond our ability observe, so they are beyond the reach of falsifiability and therefore more likely to be repeated.

As humans increased their stock of knowledge, they undertook more complex behaviors and therefore had more complex things to teach their children. This naturally selected for traits that made us better storytellers. As better storytellers, we were able to build more effectively on prior accumulated knowledge. This created even more content and therefore additional evolutionary return to reinforcing traits that supported storytelling.

The importance of storytelling might also shed light on why humans live so long and have such large brains. The most common explanation for why humans live long is that grandparents can help raise children. But that does not explain why most humans can live well after their grandchildren become adults.

Old people serve as libraries of knowledge. Teaching children and young adults how the world works and teaching young adults and middle-aged adults how to raise children is what the old people of every society do. It is in their genes because without such an inclination, our expensive brains wouldn't be worth preserving so long.

As we evolved traits that made us better storytellers, we had more knowledge to convey to the next generation. Genes cannot convey complex ideas, but complex ideas are often valuable. With the rise of language, each successive generation had a richer base of such ideas to work from. This increased the evolutionary return to having more memory capacity to store ideas and more processing power to understand increasingly abstract, complex, and subtle ideas. This process fed on itself to produce ever bigger brains.[8]

Some stories convey beliefs about right and wrong. If stories about right and wrong help reduce opportunism, then they can increase trust and therefore increase the scale and scope of cooperation. The stories a society passes from generation to generation are a part of its culture and a reflection of the power of culture to foster cooperation through moral beliefs that benefit the group. In the words of Charles Darwin in *Descent of Man* (1871, chapter 5):

> A high standard of morality gives but a slight or no advantage to each individual man and his children over the other men of the same tribe, yet . . . an increase in the number of well-endowed men and an advancement in the standard of morality will certainly give an immense advantage to one tribe over another. A tribe including many members who . . . were always ready to aid one another, and to sacrifice themselves for the common good, would be victorious over most other tribes; and this would be natural selection.

The Cultural Commons Dilemma

The set of stories told and retold in a society is effectively owned in common by the members of that society. They are therefore a common asset. The better the job these stories do producing societal success, the more valuable this common asset is to society.

In most societies culture improves efficiency by providing a basis for social harmony through practices that are imitated and through beliefs that are learned through stories. In some societies culture conveys moral beliefs that are particularly good at producing trustworthy individuals even in large-group contexts. This supports a tremendous scale and scope of cooperation and therefore mass flourishing.

For a high-trust society, such trust-producing moral beliefs are obviously a thing of great common value to everyone. Such beliefs constitute a kind of cultural commons. The metaphor of the cultural commons highlights that there are two significant problems associated with sustaining trust-producing culture. In short, the cultural commons can be ruined from abuse and it can be ruined from neglect.

Abusing the Commons

In 1968 Garrett Hardin wrote a famous essay titled "The Tragedy of the Commons." Borrowing from an example first employed by William Forster Lloyd in 1883, Hardin explained why a common pasture is prone to being ruined from overgrazing. His goal was to lay out the basic logic of what is now known in game theory as *the commons dilemma*. In doing so he hoped to demonstrate why the problem of overpopulation is so daunting and would therefore likely require the exercise of government power to solve it.

Hardin called the tragedy of the commons a "commonize costs–privatize profits" game. That game is now viewed as a specific example of what game theorists call the commons dilemma problem. These kinds of problems are prevalent in large societies and they are hard to solve. They are not the result of stupidity or irrationality. Most cannot be solved by creating rules against socially ruinous behavior even if everyone endorses the rules and agrees to obey them.

The reason why commons dilemma problems are so hard to solve is that they are the result of perfectly rational behavior. A central tenet of economics is that individually rational behavior is normally consistent with promoting the common good. But when the benefits and the costs of actions are not realized by the same decision-maker, a wedge is driven between the common good and that which most benefits the individual.

Consider Hardin's common pasture. Suppose there is an amount of total grazing that best promotes the common good, so the village establishes a rule limiting grazing to achieve that result. If we set aside morality, then the problem is that in all but the smallest villages such a level of grazing will not be achieved because such a rule will not be followed. This is true even if everyone agrees with the wisdom of the rule. This is because each individual knows he can do even better if he overgrazes a little while everyone else follows the rule.

The crux of the problem is that the benefit of breaking the rule is enjoyed solely by the opportunist, while the cost of doing so is shared by the entire village. In this case, the benefit to the opportunistic farmer is that his cows get to eat an additional bushel of grass. The cost is that this leaves one less bushel of grass in the common to be shared by all farmers tomorrow. If there are n farmers, the cost to the opportunistic farmer is therefore 1/nth of one bushel less grass available for his cows to graze on tomorrow. This makes disobeying the rule attractive for any farmer, and the larger is n, the more attractive disobedience will be. This kind of problem is so prevalent that long ago economists gave it a name: the 1/nth problem.

This strong incentive to renege on an agreed level of grazing produces a paradoxical result. If morality is ignored—that is, if the rational promotion of self-interest is all that drives decision-making—then each farmer will rationally act to improve his welfare by breaking the rule if he thinks it very unlikely that he will be caught. But when they all do so, they all end up worse off because the common pasture is then ruined. Behavior that is individually rational therefore produces an outcome that is inferior for the community. This is called a dilemma because the behavior involved is perfectly rational for the decision-makers involved, so there appears to be no rational way out of the problem.

We naturally suspect that a small common pasture shared by only a few farmers is not likely to be ruined by overgrazing. Three farmers can easily devise the kind of communal solution that Elinor Ostrom documented in her work.[9] It's easy to keep an eye on just two other farmers that use the same 150-acre common pasture. Even if one could get away with cheating, the benefit derived from doing so would likely harm the other two enough to arouse suspicion. And since actual farmers are not likely to be completely amoral, their innate moral reluctance to harm others would also likely arouse feelings of guilt for having harmed their neighbors noticeably.

But what about a 10,000-acre common used by 200 farmers? This is the same number of acres per farmer, but sheer size produces an important difference. Sheer size drives the effect of a little more grazing by one farmer on the whole commons to essentially zero. It is almost certain no one will even notice if a little more grass is eaten, so the innate moral reluctance to harm others will be rendered moot. But this is true for all farmers from the village, so they all do it, and because they all do it, the common pasture is slowly but surely ruined. As we consider ever larger villages and common pastures, the wedge between individual welfare and the common good widens, so the problem worsens.

How does Hardin's common pasture relate to the cultural commons? In the cultural commons, each untrustworthy act amounts to taking advantage of the high-trust society that has been built up over the years. The benefit of doing so for any citizen might be great, but the harm done to a large, high-trust society is often imperceptible. Just as one more bushel of grass does not noticeably degrade a large common pasture, one more act of untrustworthiness does not destroy a large, high-trust society's trust conventions or noticeably change its level of total output.

Suppose you discover a chance to exaggerate a tax deduction with no chance of being caught to get an additional refund of $500. The benefit to you is having another $500 to spend. In a society of 25 persons, this act would cost each individual $20. This might be noticed, and even if it wasn't, your innate moral reluctance to harm others would likely lead you to expect to feel guilty for having done noticeable harm to others.

But things are very different for a large society like the United States. In the United States the cost to other individuals is roughly $500/325 million people ≈ 0.0001 percent per individual. This is obviously too small to be noticed and will not produce guilt due to harming another person. So the cultural commons of a large society is far more likely to suffer from trust-eroding opportunism than the cultural commons of a small society.

More generally, if the rational promotion of self-interest is unbridled by moral restraint, then everyone will act on all golden opportunities.[10] This is the very definition of an untrustworthy person. In large societies especially, this ruins the cultural commons because when individuals behave in an untrustworthy way, they enjoy all of the benefit from doing so while bearing little or no cost. And even if individuals possess a measure of moral restraint from their innate moral reluctance to harm others, the cost of experiencing feelings of guilt will also be driven to nearly zero because there will be little or no harm done to those with whom these individuals can empathize.

This is devastating because such completely rational opportunism makes it irrational for people to presume that others are trustworthy. This destroys the high-trust society, which drives up transaction costs directly because we can't trust each other. It also drives up transaction costs indirectly by making it impossible to sustain highly trust-dependent institutions.

For some time the effect of group size on trust was largely overlooked in theoretical and empirical work because trust was typically framed in small-group terms. Even when using large samples of anonymous subjects, trust was still modeled in bilateral fashion. This meant the harm done to B from A's taking advantage of B is fully or mostly borne by B, so the guilt A would expect to feel from harming B would be significant even if B were a stranger, because our ability to empathize makes us think of even strangers as individual persons whose lives matter.

More recent work considers the effect of group size on trust, and some of it takes care not to model trust in bilateral fashion.[11] Broadly, the evidence shows that trust behavior weakens with group size, which obviously presents a problem for societies that hope to benefit from large-group cooperation. People appear to prefer limiting trust to small groups where they can most rationally count on others' unwillingness to harm them. This suggests that overcoming the commons dilemma is likely to be very hard for large societies.

Neglecting the Commons

The most obvious example of how a common pasture's upkeep might be neglected would be failing to adequately fertilize it.

Similarly, a high-trust society's upkeep might be neglected by failing to adequately cultivate prosocial behaviors and moral values, since individuals who possess these qualities are more likely to be good people who will provide a better start for building a good society, all else the same. But as concerning as this form of neglect is for a high-trust society, it pales in comparison to neglecting to invest adequate resources into combating the abuse problem.

Fertilizing to increase the productivity of a common pasture is futile if overgrazing is out of control. A village cannot spread enough fertilizer to beat an overgrazing problem any more than an individual can earn enough money to beat an overspending problem. A farmer who is willing to break the rules will just graze more cattle when increased fertilizing produces more grass per acre. Similarly, making better people by cultivating prosocial behaviors and moral values is equally futile if opportunism in general and untrustworthy behavior in particular are not strongly suppressed.

Suppose a firm has expensive machine tools that are frequently stolen. Buying better machine tools or buying them at a faster rate will not solve the problem, it will likely make it worse. What is needed is investment of resources into combating theft, in addressing the abuse directly, by, for example, investing resources into security personnel to protect the machine tools that increase productivity in a manufacturing firm. No amount of investment into machine tools that *can* increase the productivity of the firm *will* actually increase the productivity of the firm if the abuse problem is not addressed.

Analogously, no amount of investment of resources invested into the cultural commons to cultivate prosocial behaviors and moral values will produce a high-trust society if the abuse problem is not adequately addressed. Lots of nice people can try to create a high-trust society by example, but if more than a small proportion of the population always acts on golden opportunities to benefit themselves at the expense of the common good, this approach cannot work. Rational people, even very nice rational people, will not extend trust to strangers if it is irrational to do so. This means that neglecting to invest adequate resources into the cultural commons to combat abuse is a more serious problem than neglecting to invest adequate resources into the cultural commons to inculcate prosocial behaviors and moral values.

Combating Abuse

Those who behave in an untrustworthy manner ruin the high-trust society just as assuredly as those who excessively graze their cows ruin Hardin's common pasture. In both cases individual rationality undermines the common good. So humans have a daunting problem to solve. The good life requires cooperating in large groups, but the larger the group, the more likely individual rationality will undermine large-group trust and therefore undermine the common good.

Understanding this does not change the outcome because individuals can only change their own behavior. For a high-trust society to exist, nearly everyone must refrain from behaving in an untrustworthy manner. The most successful societies are those that have most effectively addressed this problem. At the same time, if a struggling society gets better at addressing this problem over time, it will become more successful.

A large society that hopes to be a high-trust society therefore needs to address the abuse problem above all else. How can this be done? What is needed is to figure out how to get nearly everyone to follow rules that maximize the common good. The larger a society is and the harder it is to enforce such rules through formal institutions, the more likely this need will come down to ensuring that nearly everyone in society is trustworthy enough to follow the rules even when there is no chance of being detected.

One way to produce this result is to have prevailing moral beliefs that produce rule following through moral restraint that results, not from a calculation of what is morally best at the point of decision, but from a belief that behaving in an opportunistic way is inherently wrong. For persons who have such beliefs, it is irrelevant that a forbidden act might bring great personal reward and noticeably harm no one.

Actually achieving this condition is very difficult. It requires investment into the inculcation of moral beliefs that have little reason to come naturally to us because in the small-group environment we evolved in, harm-based moral restraint was normally sufficient to produce adequate trust. Large-group trust is superfluous in small groups, so ideas pertinent to large-group trust but not small-group trust have had no reason to be reinforced by cultural natural selection. Moreover, in chapter 5 I will explain why it is that if a society got so lucky as to stumble onto moral beliefs that can support large-group trust and everyone in society abided by such beliefs, such beliefs necessarily have characteristics that will lead to inadequate investment to produce a high-trust society.

But the main point here is that only if the abuse problem is addressed by investing adequately into the inculcation of moral beliefs that can produce trustworthiness in large-group contexts does it becomes worthwhile for a society to invest in prosocial behaviors and moral values, as well as building up the kind of virtues discussed by Aristotle, Max Weber, and Deirdre McCloskey. The societies that adequately address the abuse problem and also invest heavily in such prosocial behaviors, moral values, and virtues are the societies that flourish the most. In the next chapter I turn to the task of outlining the kinds of moral beliefs that best address the abuse problem in large-group contexts.

Notes

1. Transactions occur to effectuate gains from cooperation and gains from exchange. Arguments made about gains from cooperative transactions apply in a straightforward way to gains from exchange.

2. See Rose (2000) and Rose (2002) for a more extensive explication of the gains from cooperation.

3. It is hard to overstate the importance of Adam Smith to our understanding of large-group cooperation. For an engaging introduction to Smith, see James Otteson's (2002) *Adam Smith's Marketplace of Life*.

4. Relational contracts are an incredibly important topic in economics. The seminal references are Macaulay (1963) and Macneil (1978). See also Baker, Gibbons, and Murphy (2002). For a discussion of their role in economic development, see Greif (1993, 2006). Over time their dependence on trust has been increasingly appreciated (see Bodoh-Creed 2017).

5. *Presumptive trust* is not absolute trust in everyone. It means that unless there is evidence to suggest someone is untrustworthy, it is rational to presume he is trustworthy. This is conditional on the circumstances involved. An individual presumed to be trustworthy enough for ordinary transactions might not be presumed trustworthy enough to deliver a bag of unmarked bills.

6. The phrase "radius of trust" comes from Francis Fukuyama in his book *Trust* (1995).

7. This is now a widely accepted principle of culture. See, for example, Boyd and Richerson (1985), Richerson and Boyd (2005), and Bowles and Gintis (2011).

8. A similar explanation for large human brains is offered by Joseph Henrich in his book *The Secret of Our Success* (2016). He gives an example of how cultural accumulation of knowledge resulted in a termite stick becoming a spear over many generations, inducing growing brain size in a positive feedback process.

9. For a discussion of her design principles for common pool resources, see her book *Governing the Commons: The Evolution of Institutions for Collective Action* (1990).

10. The concept of a "golden opportunity" was introduced by Robert Frank in his book *Passions within Reason* (1988). A golden opportunity is a chance to behave opportunistically with no chance of being caught.

11. For a recent and very exhaustive review of existing literature in this area as well as new empirical work on the effect of group size that controls for a variety of factors, see La Macchia et al. (2016).

3

Culture as Moral Beliefs

The cultural commons of a high-trust society is prone to being degraded by the very people who benefit from it. This is because there are powerful, rational incentives for individuals to behave in untrustworthy ways. In the last chapter I explained why this problem cannot be solved by declaring it "socially irrational" and then imploring people to act rationally, because they are already acting rationally.

This seems to suggest that to have a high-trust society, we need people to behave irrationally. But irrational individuals will be at a disadvantage when competing with rational individuals in any given society. Moreover, societies dominated by irrational individuals will be at a disadvantage when competing with societies dominated by rational individuals. How, then, can a society overcome the abuse problem without undermining rationality generally?

In this chapter I explain why moral beliefs about right and wrong are the key to overcoming this rationality problem and therefore addressing the problem of abuse of the cultural commons.[1] Moral beliefs can channel the ends to which rationality is directed in a way that can create and sustain a high-trust society while preserving rational decision-making and scientific inquiry. Robert Frank (1988) took the first step in explaining how this works by showing why trustworthiness must be derived from moral tastes. I will extend his argument to identify the kind of moral tastes that best support trustworthiness and the kind of moral beliefs that best instantiate those moral tastes.

We are understandably reluctant to discuss differences in the content of moral beliefs across societies. But what follows is not an endorsement of any ideology or religion. What turns out to matter most is not the list of moral values or how moral the average individual is. What turns out to matter most is how moral beliefs logically structure the relationship between moral values that are shared by people in most societies, because this governs how people *think about* morality.

My approach here is therefore quite different from that of Deirdre McCloskey. In three books and several papers, she has explained how specific virtues spurred the rise of capitalism. This is an important part of the story of the rise of mass flourishing. I focus instead on the way moral beliefs logically structure the relationship between simpler moral values that vary little across societies to produce a high-trust society that serves as fertile ground for free market democracy.[2]

Why Beliefs Matter

Beyond Cultural Practices

A hallmark of a high-trust society is people readily extending trust to one another, even strangers, because they believe there is little risk in doing so. This is partly a matter of rational decision-making, partly a matter of habit, and partly a matter of sheer imitation. Undoubtedly much of what accounts for individuals readily trusting others in any high-trust society is simply habit that began with imitation.

Although our innate predilection to imitate prevailing norms helps reinforce the practice of extending trust, that practice would end quickly if it produced inferior outcomes. It begins because people observe that when others extend trust, doing so nearly always produces a benefit because trusters are almost never victimized by others. It continues as long as untrustworthiness is rare enough to ensure that a willingness to extend trust remains a good bet.

Some have viewed trust behavior as a convention without recognizing that the extension of trust must be grounded in the rational expectation of trustworthiness.[3] But there is now a strong consensus that a durable convention of extending trust without a norm of trustworthiness is impossible. Hardin (2002), Levi (1998), Ostrom (2003), Ahn and Ostrom (2003), Gneezy (2005), Rose (2011), and others have argued that the extension of trust must be based on the rational expectation of trustworthiness. Extending trust to frequently untrustworthy transaction partners ensures worse outcomes. People learn quickly from this experience or suffer the consequences. A convention of automatically extending trust in most circumstances to strangers therefore requires a norm of trustworthiness. So what gives rise to a norm of trustworthiness?

Innate versus Invented Moral Beliefs

It should surprise no one that social scientists tend to focus their attention on developing highly general theories of how culture works. This is evidenced by numerous efforts to explain morality and trust in terms of evolutionary psychology. This approach has much to recommend it.

Moral behavior is based on many factors, and some of these factors are almost certainly innate. It is also clear that in all human groups there are highly trustworthy people. Moreover, even those who sometimes behave in untrustworthy ways usually believe that being untrustworthy is wrong, and they are trustworthy in most other circumstances. This suggests that a capacity for trustworthiness is part of our basic human nature.

The problem is that our basic human nature arose in a social context that is inadequate for supporting the kind of cooperation needed to produce general prosperity. Mass flourishing requires general prosperity. That requires making the most of large-group cooperation, which requires large-group trust. But nearly all of our evolution took place in small groups.

So while trust is plentiful, the innate traits that we all share are traits that well support trust in the context of small groups. This explains why most people in *all* societies are normally trustworthy and willing to extend trust in small-group contexts like families or neighborhoods. It also explains why trust behavior is so prevalent in economic experiments in *all* societies even when it is irrational in the context of the game being played.[4]

Why is irrational behavior so prevalent in trust games? The answer is that most of these games are framed in a small-group context, which actuates small-group trust mechanisms. For example, in a trust game in which the subject interacts with one other person, the subject can envision that person even if he is a total stranger. He can therefore empathize with that total stranger. This leads the subject to sympathize with the other player's plight and therefore refrain from driving an unfair bargain or failing to reciprocate an act made in good faith.

This means that what appears to be irrational behavior is actually quite rational. It only appears irrational because we ignore expected guilt costs. There is nothing irrational about being unwilling to do something that you expect to feel guilty about because you believe it to be morally wrong according to your moral beliefs and intuitions. Most of us have an innate moral reluctance to harm other individuals, even if they are strangers, and we find those who don't feel such reluctance to be terrifying.

In any case, a great deal of prior scholarly work essentially looks for the kind of trust behavior that is the most prevalent in the world, which is necessarily based on traits we all share. Such work then finds such trust in ample supply to the chagrin of hardcore rational theorists. But this is not the kind of trust that can work in large groups. It is based on mechanisms that evolved in a small-group context. These mechanisms, such as harm-based moral restraint arising from expecting to feel guilty about harming other individuals with whom we empathize, are often irrelevant in large-group contexts because harm is spread over a great many people.

But unlike genes, institutions do vary greatly across societies. Many have therefore argued that differences in societal success are mostly explained by differences in institutions. But if that is true, why don't all societies adopt the institutions of societies that enjoy mass flourishing? One could answer by saying that changing institutions is not that easy because a given institutional environment can suffer from lock-in. This is a good point, but is it not hard to imagine that this could happen in truly high-trust society? And doesn't this beg the question of why such lock-in exists in the first place?

Others have argued that once some level of trade gets going, trustworthiness is rewarded. This increases the returns to being trustworthy, which induces greater investment into trustworthy traits. This lowers transaction costs and thereby spurs more trade, and so on. But if that were true, the oldest commercial societies should be the highest-trust societies, and many aren't. As I have argued earlier, many institutions are themselves highly trust dependent, so it seems more likely that something more fundamental produces high-trust societies and that this something, in turn, makes highly trust-dependent institutions possible.

Humans have a large cerebral cortex capable of inventing beliefs that can differ greatly across groups. Our dramatic differences in quality of life comport with dramatic differences in beliefs that are very consistent within any given society but vary greatly across societies. I submit that in some societies invented beliefs provide a basis for trust that can be sustained in large-group contexts. While human genes vary little from group to group, the belief systems they make possible vary greatly because they are constructed, not encoded.

Unlike genes, moral beliefs vary enough to explain the differential success of societies. Although the desire to find explanations that are applicable to all humans in all societies is understandable, this approach will almost certainly be incapable of explaining differences between societies. Sheer logic dictates that one cannot explain differences between societies by something they all have in common.

How Moral Beliefs Create High-Trust Societies

The Rationality Problem

Robert Frank, in his book *Passions within Reason* (1988), explained why if the only reason a person does not behave opportunistically is that it is in his best interest not to do so, he will act on every golden opportunity that comes along. This is because the very logic that produces restraint when there is some chance of detection compels opportunism when there is no chance of detection. Rational restraint alone therefore cannot produce trustworthiness in precisely those situations that most require genuine trustworthiness.

The Moral Taste Solution

Frank was the first to clearly identify the rationality problem as the major obstacle to trust. He essentially argued that the solution is to go upstream of rational analysis in the decision-making process to effectuate moral restraint through tastes. This works because moral tastes are taken as given before rational analysis commences.

Frank's point can be extended. By effectuating moral restraint through tastes rather than enlightened self-interest, a society can beat the rationality problem without calling for irrationality or suppressing rationality in a general way. The trick is to use tastes to channel rationality and thereby govern the ends to which rationality is directed. This preserves rationality because there is nothing inherently irrational about abiding one's tastes.

For example, many people enjoy peanuts even though eating them is fattening. But even people who are struggling to lose weight sometimes eat peanuts. Does this make them irrational? Of course not. Their taste for peanuts is a prerational part of the decision-making process. Liking peanuts is neither rational nor irrational. Rationality is about being effective at getting what you like; it is not about what you like.

Genuine trustworthiness can be produced by instantiating moral tastes that make people unwilling to behave in an untrustworthy way. Frank argued that the trick to producing trustworthiness is to use moral tastes to produce involuntary feelings of guilt that the decision-maker will expect to experience even if undetected. If the psychic cost of experiencing such feelings of guilt is sufficiently high, then acting on a golden opportunity becomes irrational.[5] This approach to producing trustworthiness can be scaled up to solve the cultural commons dilemma problem. By instantiating moral tastes that can be expected to produce strong and involuntary feelings of guilt upon behaving in an untrustworthy way across all members of a society, a society can more closely align every individual's interests with the common good.

Frank was the first to recognize that moral tastes provided a way around the rationality problem associated with golden opportunities. But Frank did not address the specific nature of those tastes other than to say that, to be effective, they must produce involuntary feelings of guilt. His focus was on the role that emotions play in signaling others that individuals have the required moral tastes to be trustworthy, so others can identify them as trustworthy transaction partners.

What Kind of Moral Tastes?

In the standard model of rational consumer choice, the concept of tastes normally pertains to preferences associated with goods in an individual's utility function.[6] Such goods can be substituted for one another if the net benefit from doing so warrants the substitution. The net benefit from consuming any given good relative to others can be affected by changes to the costs involved. Suppose a person believes that a hamburger is a good substitute for a slice of pizza. In this case a reduction in the price of hamburgers might induce that person, who was about to buy a slice of pizza, to buy a hamburger instead.

As powerful as the model of rational choice is, applying it to moral values is problematic. If moral tastes simply function like tastes associated with goods in the model of rational consumer choice, then positive moral actions like giving money to a poor person and negative moral actions like embezzling from an employer are treated like things that can be substituted for one another, like a hamburger for a slice of pizza. In such a case a person's level of morality is determined by the extent to which positive moral actions outweigh negative moral actions.

But this means that if a positive moral action requires taking a negative moral action as a means to that end, and the former carries greater moral weight than the latter, then one's well-being will be increased by taking that negative moral action even though one believes taking the negative moral action is wrong. This is a well-known shortcoming of the simplest utilitarian approaches to moral ethics.

The economic model of rational choice is normally presented through the mathematics of constrained optimization. These models have two parts: (1) what is being maximized (for an individual this is utility[7]), and (2) anything that impedes such maximization. The first part is called the objective function, and the second part is called the constraint function.

In the standard model, tastes enter the story through the utility function. A typical utility function would be

$$U = X^{\alpha} Y^{\beta} Z^{\gamma},$$

where U is the level of utility and the variables X, Y, and Z are things that affect utility. The absolute values of α, β, and γ reflect the strength of the individual's tastes regarding X, Y, and Z, respectively. A positive value for α means that more X will increase utility.

Suppose that X pertains to a good that can be consumed to produce happiness and Y pertains to a positive moral action, like giving money to a poor person. The more an individual values being moral, the larger β will be relative to α. When the model is mathematically solved, it will be clear that a larger β will result in more of the positive moral action Y.

Suppose that Z pertains to a negative moral action like behaving in an untrustworthy way. If the individual values being moral, γ will be negative, so increasing Z will result in experiencing guilt, which reduces well-being. An increase in the absolute value of γ will therefore make the individual less likely to behave in an untrustworthy way, all else the same.

We naturally think of morality as a struggle between good and evil, between positive and negative moral action, and therefore between positive and negative moral values. This leads us to naturally conclude that if we want people not to behave in an untrustworthy way, we must drive up the strength of distaste associated with untrustworthy behavior, which in our simple model means to make sure that γ is both negative and very large in absolute value. It is certainly true that such an approach increases trustworthy behavior in many contexts. But this approach can run into trouble, especially in large-group settings, for two reasons.

The Empathy Problem

We normally don't behave in untrustworthy ways because we know we will feel guilty if we harm someone else. Our innate moral reluctance to harm others is very strong and universal, so our innate sense of moral restraint is almost certainly accurately characterized as harm-based moral restraint. But what if a person, or those he cares about, can benefit greatly from behaving in an untrustworthy way without actually harming anyone?

If one's moral beliefs equate wrongfulness with harmfulness, then doing something like cheating on income taxes will not feel wrong because the harm is spread over so many people that there is no individual with whom to empathize, sympathize, and therefore feel guilty about harming. Even the poorest person cannot perceive of less than one cent of harm, and we saw in chapter 2 that far less than one cent of harm is done to any American when one individual increases his refund by $500 by cheating on his tax return.

This is a very common problem in large societies because people are frequently in situations in which, because no one is noticeably harmed by a proscribed act, they can personally benefit without feeling they've done wrong. Taking home a few reams of paper from your office saves you money, but not one of your employer's owners is hurt by even one cent. In such a case, if you are certain you will not be caught, why not?

Solving the Empathy Problem

The trick to solving the empathy problem is to attach feelings of guilt directly to negative moral actions by cultivating the belief that some actions are wrong as a matter of principle. In this case, even if someone knows that cheating on taxes or taking home reams of paper will noticeably harm no one, he will still expect to feel guilty. If the expected cost of feeling guilty is so high that it outweighs the expected gain, the individual will not cheat even if he is certain that he will not be detected and that no one will be noticeably harmed. Societies that want to enjoy the benefits of large-group trust should therefore teach moral beliefs that tie guilt directly to negative moral actions to produce what might be called *principled moral restraint*.

The Greater-Good Rationalization Problem

Suppose an individual knows he will feel guilty if he does not undertake a specific positive moral action, like giving money to a poor person. Suppose this individual can only undertake this action by taking a negative moral action. If the guilt he expects to feel from undertaking this negative moral act is less than the guilt he expects to feel from failing to undertake the positive moral act, it will be rational for him to undertake the negative moral act.

This mode of moral reasoning is perfectly natural. Taking the negative moral action as a means to the end of taking the positive moral action will feel morally right in the decision-maker's gut. We evolved brains that perform cost-benefit analysis informed by an acute sense of empathy for those around us. The traits involved were reinforced over time because in the small-group milieu within which they evolved this approach to decision-making was very efficient. But if people in society make a habit of engaging in such greater-good rationalizations, the belief that others can be trusted in nearly all circumstances will be undermined, and eventually the presumptive extension of trust will become irrational for a wide variety circumstances.[8]

Another problem is that when our means of determining what is moral involves balancing expected moral costs and expected moral benefits, it inevitably produces social insularity. This is because the estimates of the moral costs and benefits involved are made in the mind of the same moral decision-maker. Because of the inherent subjectivity of these estimates, they will likely be affected by the nature of the parties involved.

One's subjective estimate of the moral benefit of an action that helps Bob is likely to be higher if Bob is a nephew, old friend, or fellow tribe member than if Bob is a complete stranger. At the same time, one's subjective estimate of the moral cost of an action that harms Sue in order to help Bob is likely to be lower if Sue is not a niece, not an old friend, and not a fellow tribe member. This means that greater-good rationalizations are prone to facilitating nepotism, cronyism, and tribalism, because it is rather easy to rationalize actions that help those we care about (or those who might help us later by returning the favor) by harming those we care little about.

As long as everyone we interact with is from the same small group, this is a minor problem. But in large groups we frequently interact with those completely unknown to us. When we expect such "others" to discount the moral cost of using us as a means to advancing their ends, we *cannot* presume them to be trustworthy in their dealings with us. Moreover, the larger the group involved, the more likely it is that harm is divided so much that there is little or no real harm to any individual, making it even easier to rationalize taking a negative moral action.

It would seem that an obvious solution would be to drive up the absolute value of γ. But this solution has a serious problem. No matter how strongly one values being trustworthy, one might also value being benevolent so strongly that in some cases morality will be viewed as being best advanced by behaving in an untrustworthy way to enable a positive moral action.

How, then, can a society ensure that moral decision-making will not be unduly affected by greater-good rationalizations? I submit that this problem requires a solution that has more to do with how moral values are logically organized in relation to each other in the belief system than the list of moral values or how badly people want to be moral.

Solving the Greater-Good Rationalization Problem

While unconventional, there is no reason why a person's utility function cannot have tastes that function like external constraints. In this case moral restraint is not produced through the relative strength of negative moral values but by effectively taking negative moral actions out of consideration. An individual is most likely to be trustworthy if he is not subject to the greater-good rationalization problem because he possesses moral tastes that effectively redact untrustworthy actions from the domain of his utility function.

The field of cognitive science suggests a plausible means by which moral tastes can, over time, come to function more like constraints than negative moral values. Suppose moral restraint is produced through feelings of guilt derived from a moral distaste for untrustworthiness, so $\gamma < 0$ in the utility function above and Z is a measure of untrustworthy acts.

An important principle of neuroscience is that neurons that fire together wire together.[9] When the same moral decision is always reached via moral cost-benefit analysis—such as that a particular kind of action will not be taken because the expected guilt costs are too high—over time this should produce a de facto constraint. This results from the withering of neural connections when they are repeatedly found to be a waste of cognitive resources. So when chances for behaving in an untrustworthy way present themselves, the neural pathway to areas of the brain involved in cost-benefit analysis weaken because the answer is always no. At the same time, neural connections that loop around cost-benefit analysis to go straight to the answer "no" are reinforced. At some point the neural connections in the loop become so strong that "no" becomes automatic.

This is very consistent with the moral development of children. Even the most trustworthy adults were calculative opportunists as small children. But, overtime, a combination of being taught that opportunism is wrong, conditioning to reinforce an automatic intuitive sense that it is wrong, and experiencing guilt from behaving in such ways, leads to declining opportunism. Over time an adult's estimate of the expected cost of experiencing guilt rises over a growing set of circumstances. So a child can start out merely *valuing* not being untrustworthy and frequently agonizing over temptation and sometimes giving in, but end up as an adult who never even considers untrustworthy actions in the course of ordinary life.

This is very different from how moral decision-making is often portrayed in economic models, but it comports well with how many adults actually behave. We all know adults who never even consider undertaking negative moral actions. I submit that these people are not winning a daily struggle against temptation. Their behavior is better viewed as moral habit that arises from their brains having long ago given up considering opportunism because doing so is a waste of time.[10]

This is a significant change in moral thinking. A constraint that manifests itself by effectively redacting the set of actions from the domain of the utility function exerts its effect prerationally. Accordingly, it is beyond the reach of the rationality problem because, as Frank pointed out, the crux of that problem is that acting on golden opportunities is always rational. But when the automatic answer "no" decides the outcome before the potential benefits are even considered, the potential benefits—even selfless benefits—do not provide a basis for temptation. There is, of course, no greater assurance that another person can always be trusted than to know he doesn't even consider behaving in an untrustworthy way.[11]

The key is to drive the *moral* decision-making process away from its natural cost-benefit mode of analysis. This is very hard to do because in the milieu in which most of our evolution took place this cost-benefit approach to moral decision-making was very efficient. Few things are as brutally consequentialist in nature as the process of natural selection. Natural selection therefore reinforced traits that favor thinking in terms of rational cost-benefit analysis. But what is optimal for the individual at the moment of individual decision-making in a small-group context is often not what is best for the common good in a large society in the long run.

Moral Beliefs That Best Instantiate the Required Moral Tastes

Moral beliefs that emphasize moral advocacy—undertaking positive moral actions—are important in their own right, but they are not necessary for getting people to do what needs to be done to maximize general prosperity. As I explained in chapter 2, transactions that produce the greatest surpluses are also the most important for achieving mass flourishing. But by their very nature they are also the most likely to be voluntarily undertaken.

Those familiar with the economic theory of market failure are likely to object to this point.

Market failure refers to instances in which the free market system fails to best promote the common good. The most common examples are externalities (e.g., pollution produced by firms that far exceeds what best promotes the common good if left to the free market) and public goods (e.g., national defense that will be woefully inadequate if left to the free market).

There is a large literature devoted to the study of market failure and how government can address it so as to maximize the common good. It is unnecessary and unwise to address market failure problems by increasing general moral earnestness or encouraging specific positive moral actions because any given positive moral action requires resources, so it necessarily comes at the expense of consumption and other positive moral actions.

For society to best promote the common good it must consider these trade-offs. Employing the theory of market failure, government provides a proven mechanism for doing this. Asking people to care more about being moral, to care more about a given issue, or to take more positive moral actions without a framework for addressing these trade-offs does not. Addressing market failure through moral advocacy therefore wastes resources by failing to direct them where they will do the most good. It is therefore best to use government to address market failure problems. I will return to the important topic of market failure in chapter 8.

At the same time, moral beliefs that emphasize moral advocacy are neither necessary nor sufficient for creating and sustaining high-trust societies. As I explained above, trustworthiness cannot be reliably produced by positive moral values that encourage positive moral acts because of the empathy problem and the greater-good rationalization problem. Trustworthiness requires that individuals be unwilling to take negative moral actions. Trustworthiness can therefore be undermined if it is possible for individuals to feel that they are morally obligated to undertake negative moral actions as means to the ends of undertaking positive moral actions.

It follows that moral beliefs that emphasize moral restraint are the key to creating a high-trust society. The less likely people are to take negative moral actions in general, the more likely they will always be trustworthy. Moral beliefs that emphasize moral restraint above all can therefore produce a norm of trustworthiness that, in turn, can support a convention of presumptively extending trust. This maximizes the scale and scope of transactions through which the gains from cooperation can be derived. This maximizes mass flourishing.

This does not mean that moral advocacy is not important. Moral advocacy promotes decency by inducing individuals to take positive moral actions. When the increase in utility arising from taking such actions outweighs the decrease in utility arising from the resources sacrificed, such actions are personally rational and produce a net improvement in social welfare.

Recall that positive moral action normally requires resources that have competing uses. If resources could have been used to undertake a different positive moral act that would have produced an even greater increase in social welfare, then the first positive moral act would not have best promoted the common good. So when moral advocacy disseminates information about the nature of competing moral causes to garner support from those who are most likely to favor a given cause, it helps people give support in ways that makes them happiest.

Because their happiness likely rises with the amount of good actually achieved, individuals will likely favor positive moral acts that do the most good. Finally, some individuals might be happier if they undertook positive moral acts, but they don't presently know that because they've never experienced how they will feel if they take positive moral acts. When moral advocates persuade people to take positive moral acts for the first time and the happiness produced from doing so proves to more than make up for the sacrifice in resources, social welfare is increased.

So moral advocacy is a very good thing for promoting the common good. For a society to enjoy mass flourishing, however, its prevailing moral beliefs must place moral advocacy in proper context. Anything that reduces moral restraint reduces our ability to create and sustain a high-trust society, and it is the high-trust society that makes us rich enough to have ample resources for positive moral action.

If prevailing moral beliefs view moral advocacy and restraint as equally important, then imperatives to take positive moral actions can undermine imperatives to never take negative moral actions. This is because people will be able to convince themselves that being moral requires behaving in untrustworthy ways as a means to the ends of undertaking laudable moral actions. But no matter how sincere is the desire to promote the common good in this way, it erodes our ability to trust each other. Because the gains from large-group cooperation are so great and since positive moral action is more easily undertaken by rich societies, undertaking negative moral actions as a means to the end of taking positive moral actions is, from the perspective of the common good, penny wise and pound foolish.

In short, a large society is most likely to also be a high-trust society if prevailing beliefs hold that moral restraint is a moral duty. The concept of duty comports well with beliefs that effectuate principled moral restraint. It also comports well with beliefs requiring that refraining from taking negative moral actions take strict precedence over endeavoring to take positive ones. Put directly, if it is sustainable mass flourishing a society seeks, then moral restraint should be viewed as a civic moral duty, while moral advocacy should be viewed as a personal moral choice.

These kinds of moral beliefs do not call for irrationality or for the suppression of rationality. What they do is channel rationality. They redirect consideration of untrustworthy action around the brain's rational cost-benefit analysis processing center and directly to the answer "no." Such trust-producing moral beliefs are the product of thousands of years of refinement. As comforting as it may be to think that one of our noblest traits is a product of our basic nature, our ability to create and sustain high-trust societies is anything but. Trust-producing moral beliefs are among our greatest achievements precisely because they are so contrary to our nature.

Notes

1. In chapter 5 I address the neglect problem associated with adequately inculcating trust-producing moral beliefs.

2. See Rose (2016) for a detailed discussion of this point.

3. See Eric Uslaner's (2002) *The Moral Foundations of Trust* for an example of such a treatment.

4. There is a great deal of variance in performance in such anthropological investigations. But in all such investigations there is still more trust and trustworthiness than predicted by the strict model of rational choice.

5. This can be viewed as providing a basis for "gut feelings" against behaving in an opportunistic manner along the lines discussed by Jonathan Haidt in his book *The Righteous Mind* (2012).

6. Utility functions are used to model rational choice. The amounts of various goods and services (economists normally just say "goods" for brevity) are plugged into an equation that computes a numerical value for the level of well-being.

7. In economics parlance, utility is a measure of an individual's welfare, broadly construed. In many contexts it can be viewed as the individual's level of happiness.

8. There are, of course, times when one should do something wrong (e.g., lie) as a means to the end of doing something good (e.g., protecting Anne Frank's family from the Nazis). But thankfully situations like this are very rare, so they are best thought of as exceptional cases. Few have difficulty recognizing them as exceptional cases. With respect to the vast majority of transactions in a free market economy, such exceptional stakes are not in play.

9. This is widely attributed to Lowel and Singer (1992) but expresses the main idea of Donald Hebb's theory of neuroscience in *The Organization of Behavior* (1949). I thank Joaquin Fuster of the Semel Institute for Neural Science and Human Behavior for pointing this out.

10. People often say, "Everyone has his price." But is this really true? There is no reason why the pain of guilt cannot be so high that even a billion dollars would not overcome it. Not many people would, for example, kill a child just to get a billion dollars.

11. This does not mean that highly trustworthy people are never tempted. In chapter 5 I explain why absolute trustworthiness is neither necessary nor efficient for a high-trust society.

4

Culture as Instrument

Culture presents a puzzle. How can something be so different from society to society while at the same time be so important to all societies? The answer to this puzzle lies in recognizing that the concept of culture has two parts: culture as content and culture as instrument.

Culture as content refers to beliefs and practices we associate with any given culture. This content varies greatly across societies and helps define them. Culture as instrument refers to the unique way that culture functions. Our capacity for culture is a profoundly important part of the evolutionary story of our species and is deeply rooted in our genes, so how culture works is similar across societies. The wide variety in cultures among societies is therefore mostly the result of differences in cultural content.

Understanding how culture works instrumentally is very important because this helps us understand the power of culture. My claim is that since culture works instrumentally in such a powerful way, cultural content can drive societies to extreme outcomes. Up until now we have focused on how culture can explain the differential success of societies by considering the effect of cultural content—specifically moral beliefs—on being able to create and sustain a high-trust society. But a consideration of culture as instrument opens up a far less pleasant side of culture, which is how cultural content can explain differential success by considering how moral beliefs and practices can impede large-group cooperation and thereby make some societies poor.

Tastes and Rationality

Unlike behavior that is largely encoded by genes (e.g., ant behavior in general or human blinking when cold air is unexpectedly blown into the eye), rational analysis considers available details about a given circumstance. This consideration is constrained by facts and logic to avoid mistakes. It has nothing to do with tastes per se but is, instead, about engaging in valid logical reasoning so tastes can be pursued to greatest effect in light of all relevant factors.

With rational analysis, tastes are the "givens" in the decision-making process. Since rational analysis can consider all available details, including details about completely new factors, it can produce new ways to deal with changing circumstances. Because of this, the scope of behavioral responses that can be derived from rational analysis can better match the parade of unpredictable circumstances that confront an individual, a group, or a society than tastes can. Rational analysis can therefore produce novel and surprising solutions that might differ markedly from established conventions and norms.

In the movie *Speed*, for example, a police officer purposely shoots a hostage in the leg to make the hostage useless to the criminal. Few would reach this conclusion instinctively. For most, gut feelings would result in a panicked concession to what the criminal demands, which allows the criminal to take the hostage with him. In most cases this might very well be the best decision. But what if the officer believes that, in this particular circumstance, if the criminal leaves with the hostage, no one will ever see the hostage alive again? If it is the hostage's life that is of paramount importance, then the most rational decision might be to shoot the hostage.

When tastes are strong they can produce very consistent behavior in a wide variety of circumstances. Consider nearly any small town in the American Midwest. A wide variety of circumstances can produce extreme anger between citizens. Such anger is hardly rare, but murder is. I submit that this is not because the people in those communities are more moral or are more rational than elsewhere. I submit that murder is simply not in the set of possible actions because the distaste for murder is so great that the brains of those who live in such towns don't waste cognitive resources actually considering it. This is an unfathomable luxury even for highly moral and rational people who live in areas like the South Side of Chicago, where the prospect of killing or being killed is sometimes very real.

Consistently refraining from murder cannot be produced by an imitated practice alone because the circumstances that lead up to hostility vary greatly and may therefore never be observed by people until they find themselves in such a circumstance. But if a distaste for murder derived from a moral belief that it is inherently wrong is very strong, then in virtually all circumstances murder will not occur because it is not even considered. There are exceptions, but such exceptional cases are so obvious that we don't even call taking a life in such cases murder (e.g., killing a uniformed enemy combatant in battle).

The consistency produced by taste-encoded behavior can increase harmony, but it also impedes adaptability. This is often problematic, especially in environments with rapidly changing conditions. For example, the smart move in a battle might be to withdraw and wait for reinforcements, but if a general believes that it is a moral duty never to yield an inch to an enemy, then the smart move will not be taken and a victory may be turned into a defeat. This is why most humans appreciate the value of rationality.

Producing consistency through tastes carries the risk of producing suffocating cultural norms, practices, and laws. Since taste-encoded behavior produces harmony that comes at the expense of diminished adaptability to changing conditions, a natural byproduct of encoding behavior through tastes is to suppress change through strict adherence to established norms, practices, and laws. This can produce societies that are insular, provincial, and xenophobic.

Rational Deviation

Often a group enjoys more success if there is consistency of some forms of behavior. Rational deviation refers to the possibility that it is often rational for an individual to deviate from norms and practices that produce consistency even when such consistency advances the common good.

Such norms need not involve matters of great moral gravity. I have a creek in my backyard. In the fall I can rake my leaves into the creek to save time and my doing so harms no one. Raking leaves into the creek is therefore not inherently immoral. But if everyone does it we are all, collectively, worse off. This is because it might clog and then flood after a heavy rain.

To avoid this problem, we all agree to not rake leaves into the creek. Note that our agreeing to such a rule turns a nonmoral issue into a moral one. Now if an individual rakes leaves into the creek, that individual is breaking his word, which is morally wrong. Even if he was not a direct party to the agreement, he knows he benefits from the arrangement, so raking leaves into the creek is effectively breaking part of the social contract. Either way, raking leaves into the creek has gone from being collectively unwise to being individually immoral.

But even if the individual now believes that raking leaves into the creek is immoral and will therefore feel some measure of guilt from doing so, it may still be rational for that individual to defect if the level of guilt is relatively low and the benefit of breaking the rule is relatively high. This temptation to defect undermines the rules that exist to promote the common good by avoiding things like flooded subdivisions.

Trustworthiness

Because of the problem of rational deviation from norms, practices, and rules that promote the common good, it follows that steadfast inflexibility is sometimes precisely what is best for society. With the exception of profoundly rare cases, this applies to trustworthiness.

If A transacts with B, A never wants to become a victim of B's opportunism. Producing trustworthiness through encoded tastes in B is therefore valuable to A because A doesn't want flexibility that might result in B's acting on golden opportunities at A's expense. This is true even if such opportunities are rooted in benevolence. This isn't just true for individuals like A, it is also true for society as a whole. Even when any specific untrustworthy act produces no measurable harm, when such untrustworthy actions are frequently rationalized they can destroy the high-trust society.

So an individual's transaction partners and society as a whole benefit from redacting from the domain of every individual's utility function all opportunistic actions. This obviously includes all untrustworthy actions.[1] If the moral beliefs that effectuate such a redaction do this and no more, the process of rational thought will be otherwise preserved. It will not reduce any individual's, organization's, or society's adaptability with respect to everything else. More likely it will actually increase adaptability and therefore the common good.

Consider a firm owned by A but managed by B. If A can completely trust B to act on the local knowledge that comes B's way so as to promote A's interest, then A can delegate to B discretion that would have otherwise been foreclosed because of fear of opportunistic exploitation. As already noted in chapter 2, one very important institution that facilitates such discretion is the relational contract, whose flexibility allows adaptation to changing circumstances and creative innovation to take advantage of new opportunities. Relational contracts are not some mere detail of economic and legal theory. They are essential for a creative and entrepreneurial society.

Paradoxically, by limiting every individual's discretion by redacting the domain of every individual's utility function to foreclose opportunism, all transaction partners, organizations, and society as a whole benefit from there being a significantly larger set of permitted actions than before. This, of course, affords significantly greater adaptability than otherwise. This is true because there is nothing to fear in leaving all other actions on the table as long as opportunism is taken off the table.

This is very different from avoiding the harm caused by opportunism through scripted responses to every conceivable circumstance. When assurance is produced in this way, all but the scripted responses are effectively redacted. Suppose there are three actions that might be taken, w, v, and z, and you must do w in a particular circumstance because it is the taste-encoded, scripted response. This is logically equivalent to forbidding v and z. But if we flip the rule around to make it about what you can't do rather than what you can, you have more flexibility—you can do *more*. Suppose the rule says you cannot do z. This leaves you the discretion to do either w or v. It follows directly that the larger is the set of possible actions, the greater is the potential cost from scripting actions and thereby foreclosing adaptability and creativity.

In a society in which prevailing moral beliefs ensure that nearly everyone has opportunistic actions redacted from their respective utility functions, it is possible to have organizations that are very large and also very entrepreneurial not just at the top, but throughout their hierarchy. This is because everyone can be trusted not to abuse the discretion made possible by relational contracts that make large and entrepreneurial organizations possible.

Think of the evolution of a species. Its evolution does not proceed through the sequential application of natural selection to one attribute at a time. Its evolution proceeds through many attributes all at the same time. By opening up the set of actions available to all decision-makers in an organization, moral restraint can open up the set of possible adaptations and thereby allow a much greater diversity of adaptations on multiple fronts. The winning approaches will be copied while the losing approaches will not. This story works best when new approaches are constantly being tried rather than when established procedures are steadfastly obeyed.

An ethic of duty-based moral restraint redacts the domain of the utility function in this way and thereby avoids throwing the baby out with the bathwater. There is no need for irrationality or the suppression of rationality; there is only the need to channel rationality by taking off the table those actions that will harm society. This stops rational action that harms society while otherwise preserving rationality so that it can advance the common good. Rationality is largely free to improve our understanding of the world and, as this process feeds on itself, a society can enjoy a rising standard of living ad infinitum.[2]

Childhood Instruction

Childhood instruction is a hallmark of the cultural transmission of beliefs and practices. The content of the instruction varies greatly across societies, but the practice of teaching children as early as possible is ubiquitous. I submit that this is because childhood instruction takes advantage of a quickly closing window of opportunity to control how an individual thinks about the world for the rest of his life. At some level nearly everyone in every society understands this.

Humans that work well together in groups live better than those who don't. This raises the stakes of childhood instruction even further because, as we will soon see, childhood instruction is the key to keeping individual rationality from undermining the high-trust society, thereby impeding large-group cooperation. Childhood instruction does this by addressing what I call the time consistency problem and what I call the universality problem. Both problems are addressed by separating the decision to have certain kinds of moral beliefs from the consequences of having them.

The Time Consistency Problem

In chapter 3 I explained how moral tastes can preclude opportunism prerationally and thereby overcome the rationality problem associated with golden opportunities. But this raises the question of where such moral tastes come from. If they are encoded in our genes or if our genes inevitably lead us to discover them introspectively, then most societies should already be high-trust societies. Abundant empirical evidence shows that this is not the case.[3]

Since moral beliefs vary across societies, it seems much more likely that the moral tastes that can overcome the rationality problem that undermines high-trust societies are instantiated by *learned* beliefs. So the question then becomes, how do we get people to learn and then abide by trust-producing moral beliefs?

It is unlikely that all a society need do is expose people to trust-producing moral beliefs. One reason why involves what economists call a *time consistency problem*. A time consistency problem involves situations in which what is viewed as being best by an individual at one point in time will be viewed differently by that same individual at another point in time. Most people are vaguely aware of this problem in their own lives. A person might, for example, never keep ice cream at home precisely because he likes it so much. He knows that if it is in the freezer, he is likely to eat more of it than is in his long-term best interest.

Thomas Schelling, who won the Nobel Prize in Economics in 2005, proposed the following illustration of the problem of time inconsistency. Schelling asked what a kidnapper would do if he got cold feet and the victim promised that if he let her go, she would not tell the authorities who he was. It would seem that if he lets her go, everybody wins.

But any rational kidnapper knows that this plan has an obvious flaw. No matter how sincere her promise was to not identify the kidnapper to the authorities, once she is safe, there is no reason not to do so. So the solution that both kidnapper and his victim prefer is not likely to happen because it is not time consistent. Unless the kidnapper knows he'll feel worse about killing her than being imprisoned for life, the kidnapper will kill his victim.

The classic example of someone recognizing his own problem with time consistency is Odysseus instructing his crew to lash him to the mast so he can hear the song of the Sirens. He had been told that while their song was incredibly beautiful, upon hearing it, he will be driven to sail his ship into the rocks that surround their island. So if he is to hear their song, he must take steps to address his time consistency problem. He did this by ordering his men to lash him to the mast and to ignore his pleas to be set free.

Consciously choosing to adopt moral beliefs that require one never to behave as an opportunist and therefore never to act on golden opportunities is clearly subject to a time consistency problem. Just as a rational person will not fail to act on a golden opportunity if he is restrained only by rational self-interest, he will not choose to have moral beliefs that foreclose acting on golden opportunities in the future if, at the time of choosing such beliefs, he is concerned only with rational self-interest. To argue that he might have chosen his moral beliefs for moral reasons is to completely miss the point, because that would mean he already has moral beliefs that produce moral restraint.

One could argue that even if an individual cares only about rational self-interest, choosing moral beliefs that foreclose acting on future golden opportunities is no less rational than deciding not to keep ice cream at home. But this is a poor analogy. When an individual does not keep ice cream at home but later wishes he had it readily available, he must then bear an additional cost of getting it in that future time period. So a salient detail in the ice cream example is that there is more than time involved. There is also a substantive change in circumstance in the later time period. Most people won't get out of bed while watching a late movie, put their clothes back on, and go to the grocery store to buy ice cream, even if they want it badly. But when it comes to acting on a golden opportunity, all relevant costs are already accounted for, by the very definition of a golden opportunity.

Moreover, personality traits like fretfulness or beliefs that keep someone out of trouble with respect to temptations that involve a chance of detection are irrelevant with respect to golden opportunities. Golden opportunities would be clear exceptions to moral rules of thumb if the moral beliefs involved were adopted solely for reasons of rational self-interest. If a person chooses to have a moral belief foreclosing opportunism to protect his future reputation from ruin, then when an outstanding golden opportunity comes along he will, with sudden logical clarity, remember why he adopted such a belief in the first place.

How Culture Solves the Time Consistency Problem

The key to having someone be trustworthy is for opportunistic actions to be redacted from the domain of the utility function. But such trustworthiness requires that moral beliefs that produce this condition be adopted for some reason other than rational self-interest. One way around this problem is to transmit these beliefs in some way other than having individuals choose them for themselves.

This brings us to an important and unique attribute of culture. The cultural transmission of beliefs and practices, especially moral beliefs and practices, normally occurs very early in life. That this happens in all societies is not a coincidence. By teaching moral beliefs early, a society separates the decision to choose moral beliefs from the consequences of having them. This circumvents the time consistency problem arising from an individual choosing to abide by trust-producing moral beliefs for reasons of rational self-interest alone, since in some circumstances in the future having such beliefs will reduce the individual's welfare.

At some level virtually all parents understand this. They know the earlier moral beliefs are taught, the less their acquisition by their children can be accurately described as rational choice and the more accurately it can be described as sheer absorption. To produce the kind of consistent behavior they desire from their children, parents teach moral beliefs while their children's brains readily absorb what they are taught. They then attempt to reinforce those beliefs through operant conditioning and example. In most societies, parents also try hard to keep their children from being exposed to competing moral beliefs.

Culture, then, functions in a way that allows one generation to determine the prevailing moral beliefs of the next generation, thereby largely removing the next generation's ability to choose moral beliefs for themselves. This sidesteps the time consistency problem by taking advantage of the fact that children cannot fully comprehend how costly it will be to abide by moral beliefs that foreclose acting on golden opportunities when they become adults.

This maximizes the chance that trust-producing moral beliefs will exert their influence on rational choice making as tastes in the minds of the adults of the next generation. This overcomes the general commons dilemma problem associated with opportunism by preempting its underlying logic. If moral tastes increase the expected cost of guilt far above the level of guilt produced by harm-based moral restraint alone, the net payoff to opportunism becomes negative so the commons dilemma associated with opportunism disappears.

This point about how culture works in intergenerational fashion is so important that it bears restatement. The cultural transmission of moral beliefs—that is, teaching them to children as early as possible—separates the decision to hold those beliefs from the costs of abiding by them. For the most part, children cannot possibly imagine the nature of the opportunities that will present themselves in adulthood or the opportunity cost of being unable to act on them. The earlier such beliefs are learned, the truer this is. *This is the key difference between culturally transmitted beliefs and beliefs that are transmitted in any other way.*

So what children learn from their parents are moral beliefs they would not have chosen for themselves. These beliefs instantiate moral tastes that function prerationally. These tastes unleash involuntary feelings of guilt upon an individual's behaving opportunistically that come to be expected by the individual. Some parents may intentionally strive to instantiate involuntary guilt responses to help their children be more moral than otherwise in adulthood. It is also possible, however, that for many parents this is simply a byproduct of teaching moral beliefs early in childhood, which parents do for no other reason than that it is a cultural norm in their society that they rather automatically imitate. To the extent that such a norm produces more steadfast durable moral restraint that benefits the individual and the group, it will be reinforced at the individual and the group level, respectively.

In either case, as described in chapter 3, over time the individual's brain will come to regard opportunistic action as unworthy of consideration. The individual's brain will literally bypass the cost-benefit calculation stage of decision-making when chances to behave opportunistically present themselves. The individual will have built up strong moral habits of mind that produce consistently trustworthy behavior.

In this unique way, culture moves behavior from the realm of rational decision-making based on the careful consideration of all available details into the realm of automatic behavior derived from tastes that exert their influence over decision-making in a prerational fashion. This account comports with Jonathan Haidt's framework, which draws attention to the importance of automatic moral thinking based on gut feelings.[4]

Now suppose that in a given society, virtually all children are taught at a very young age that any act of opportunism is terribly wrong even if no one is harmed. Suppose this is taught in the absence of competing moral beliefs, in conjunction with adult examples, and with reinforcing operant conditioning. In that society, a very high proportion of children will grow up to be adults who believe strongly that acting opportunistically is very wrong. Nearly everyone will be trustworthy in nearly every circumstance, so nearly everyone rationally extends trust to nearly everyone else nearly all the time.

Teaching beliefs to an individual before he or she is old enough to meaningfully choose them is a disturbing proposition. It is, essentially, an effort to engage in mind control. But it comports with the Herculean efforts adults in all societies already put toward early, vigorous, and often exclusive acculturation of their children. Moreover, some kinds of mind control, such as inculcating trust-producing moral beliefs early in childhood, do a much better job than others eliminating incentives to promote one's individual welfare at the expense of the common good in adulthood.

The Universality Problem

The more consistently a belief is held or a practice is obeyed within a group relative to its variability across groups, the more likely it will be recognized as a cultural marker for that group. Conversely, beliefs or practices that are common in a given group but that fall far short of being universally obeyed within the group are more likely to be viewed as rationally directed behavior explained by either differences in circumstances or differences in tastes across individuals.

Culture can produce consistency of behavior through consistently held beliefs. As I have already argued, consistency does not arise from sheer rationality applied to personal tastes. Consistency arises from rationality applied to tastes that reflect a given set of shared beliefs. When a very high percentage of people in a society share a given set of beliefs with great conviction, they think and behave in ways that can be relied upon by others in that it will be rational for others to presume that they will think and behave in certain ways. This can create a common basis for thinking about right and wrong.

How Culture Solves the Universality Problem

Becoming a high-trust society requires that the proportion of the population that is highly trustworthy surpasses a tipping point at which it becomes rational to *presume* that most people can be trusted in all but the most exceptional of circumstances.[5] It follows that an important factor in creating and sustaining a high-trust society is teaching trust-producing moral beliefs to a very high proportion of the population.

At the same time, everything an individual learns frames all subsequent learning. The older a person is when he learns moral beliefs, the greater will be the variety of beliefs he will be exposed to and therefore the greater will be the variation across individuals in moral beliefs as well as in their understanding of any particular moral belief system. Moreover, the younger children are when they learn any kind of belief or practice, the more likely they will learn it without distraction from other beliefs or practices, which helps ensure consistency. It follows that another important factor in creating and sustaining a high-trust society is teaching trust-producing moral beliefs as early in childhood as possible.

This may also help explain why most religions stress early childhood instruction in matters of religious doctrine. Even if it is not the intent of religious leaders to minimize the variety of learned moral beliefs to ensure consistency or to foreclose exposure to competing religions, the cultural practice of teaching religion early in childhood might nevertheless be reinforced over time because it increases doctrinal consistency and durability and thereby increases the likelihood of success for any given religion.

Culture is essentially what we already call the transmission of nongenetic information from generation to generation that is broad enough and early enough to produce highly consistent behavior within a society. This nongenetic information—cultural content—can be very different across societies, so culture varies greatly from society to society. But the practice of childhood instruction is almost universal across societies.

Parents who want their children always to behave in trustworthy ways do not put their faith in philosophical arguments their children will learn in adulthood. They teach their children so early in life that the beliefs conveyed are better described as being absorbed than being chosen. Societies throughout most of human history have also put their faith in childhood instruction, in what is better described as indoctrination. To ensure strong indoctrination, many even created institutions for systematic and early education of children in matters of right and wrong. It was Charles Darwin, after all, who said, "The highest possible stage in moral culture is when we recognize that we ought to control our thoughts" (Darwin 1871, chapter 4)

But won't individuals who don't share such moral beliefs also benefit from the presumptive extension of trust? They will, and this may lead them and their descendants to enjoy an evolutionary advantage at the expense of the majority. This advantage would naturally increase their proportion of the population over time. But if the majority understands this problem, it will appreciate the need for trust-producing moral beliefs to be universal. And in many societies, there is indeed intense pressure to conform to the approved set of moral beliefs.

This does not mean that there cannot be heterogeneity of religions in a high-trust society. Many religions are consistent with trust-producing moral beliefs because trust-producing moral beliefs work at a different level of generality than most religions. Most religions focus as much on the specific story of where moral beliefs come from as they do on the nature of those beliefs. They also focus on religious rituals that differentiate one religion from others. With respect to actions that are relevant to economic activity in large-group contexts, most religions encourage the same positive moral actions and discourage the same negative moral actions. What makes trust-producing moral beliefs different is how they logically organize the relationship of moral values to one another, which receives far less attention in most religions. I will return to this important issue in chapter 8.

Like the time consistency problem, the universality problem is also best addressed through childhood instruction. This is because the earlier one learns moral beliefs, the more likely the values they convey will function as tastes and, hence, exert their influence in prerational fashion. This produces strong consistency of behavior, which is the key to supporting the rational and presumptive extension of trust, the cultural foundation of any high-trust society.

Cultural Lock-In

Culture derives much of its power from encoding behavior through tastes that exert their influence at a prerational stage of decision-making. This means cultural content can potentially be expressed in rather extreme fashion. This can be a very good thing. In some societies, for example, virtually all people might not even consider behaving in an opportunistic manner. So cultural content like trust-producing moral beliefs combined with culture's ability to work through tastes that function prerationally can go a long way toward producing heaven on earth.

But this can also be a very bad thing. In some societies, for example, virtually all people may view anyone outside their immediate family or tribe as little more than potential dupes, as mere means to ends. So cultural content like moral beliefs that stoke tribalism combined with culture's ability to work through tastes that function prerationally can also go a long way toward producing hell on earth.

Because of how culture works instrumentally, culture can have the effect of insulating cultural content from rational scrutiny. This can produce cultural lock-in. In short, much cultural content receives little consideration by adults because it is taken as self-evident truth about the nature of the world. Being upstream of rational analysis, moral tastes are normally not subjected to the process of rational analysis. At first this sounds like good news, since cultural lock-in with respect to trust-producing moral beliefs would benefit society greatly. But in chapters 5 and 7 we will see why cultural lock-in is not likely to be enough to ensure that high-trust societies will be stable.

Unfortunately, cultural lock-in is more likely to exist with respect to other kinds of moral beliefs, including those that are inimical to the high-trust society and to free market democracies. Childhood instruction ensures that moral beliefs that are inimical to free market democracy are ingrained as moral tastes long before adulthood. Adult adherence to such beliefs is therefore derived from resolve that, while not irrational, is nevertheless prerational.

Such beliefs are often more likely to comport with our innate moral intuitions than trust-producing moral beliefs. So there is little chance of convincing the majority in such societies of the benefits of adopting moral beliefs that better support mass flourishing. In many cases, such adults may even object to the premise that mass flourishing is a worthy societal objective.

The kind of moral beliefs that best promote the common good and thereby make the good life possible require a great deal of investment, are strongly subject to erosion over time, and are therefore in constant need of costly attention. This is hardly a case of cultural lock-in. But we will see in chapters 5 and 7 why the kind of moral beliefs that put the individual, his family, and his tribe ahead of the common good are more likely to be subject to cultural lock-in because they are less subject to erosion than trust-producing moral beliefs. In this way understanding culture as instrument helps one see how cultural content can explain the persistence of oppression and poverty in some societies.

Those who are lucky enough to live in thriving free market democracies should therefore be humble about their good fortune. They owe much of their personal success to the success of the society around them. Much of that success comes from being lucky enough to live in a society in which nearly everyone abides by moral beliefs that make the high-trust society. For the most part they did not choose these beliefs; they absorbed them from those who sacrificed much to ensure they learned them well, so they can hardly take credit for having them.

Notes

1. Untrustworthiness and opportunism are not equivalent. There was nothing opportunistic about lying to the Nazis to protect Anne Frank's family. Quite the contrary. This is why nearly everyone understands that there was no genuine moral dilemma in this case.

2. This is the view of endogenous growth theory in economics. For a broad and accessible introduction to this literature, see Romer (1994).

3. Measured levels of trust and trustworthiness in large-group contexts, particularly with regard to strangers, vary greatly across countries. As but one example from a large recent study using data taken from the World Values Survey (2014), Ortiz-Ospina and Roser (2017) find that

in countries such as Norway, Sweden and Finland, more than 60% of respondents think that people can be trusted. And in the other extreme, in countries such as Colombia, Brazil, Ecuador and Peru, less than 10% think that this is the case. Notice that even in some relatively homogeneous regions, such as Western Europe, there are some marked differences: there is a twofold difference between France and neighboring Germany.

4. See note 5 in chapter 3.

5. The concept of a tipping point is important for understanding many social phenomena. See Malcolm Gladwell's book *The Tipping Point* (2000). See also Thomas Schelling (1978) and Mark Granovetter (1978).

5

The Rise of Flourishing Societies

What leads to the rise of flourishing societies? I have already explained why cooperating ever better in ever larger groups is necessary for maximizing mass flourishing and why cooperating well in large groups requires large-group trust. It follows that flourishing societies begin to rise with the rise of beliefs and practices that produce large-group trust.

It is natural to conjecture that some societies might stumble onto beliefs and practices that happen to support large-group trust. This, in turn, might lead to a norm of extending trust to others in presumptive fashion. One can imagine this norm giving such a society an advantage over another, which is then absorbed or destroyed. This spreads trust-producing beliefs and practices as memes. In this chapter I explain why, as nicely as this conjecture comports with a standard biological story of natural selection, stumbling upon trust-producing beliefs and practices is unlikely to take a society very far down the path toward becoming a high-trust society.

The first problem is that moral beliefs that come most naturally to us are derived from our innate moral intuitions, which are small-group moral intuitions. Small-group trust is therefore natural and plentiful in the world, but this also means that behaving in an untrustworthy way in large-group contexts is also natural. Recall that both the empathy problem and the greater-good rationalization problems associated with how we naturally make moral decisions intensify with group size. So even if a society stumbled on to trust-producing moral beliefs and practices, just as gravity pulls a jet airplane flying overhead to the ground, our innate small-group moral intuitions will immediately start to pull down a nascent high-trust society.

The inculcation of trust-producing moral beliefs must also overcome some very strong economic incentives. In this chapter I will explain why trust-producing moral beliefs are inherently public goods (defined below). As such, the level of investment that is rationally chosen by parents will normally be far too low to create or sustain a high-trust society.

So stumbling onto trust-producing moral beliefs is not nearly enough for a society to become a high-trust society that supports mass flourishing. Even if every adult knows, understands, and strongly abides by trust-producing moral beliefs, the deck is still stacked against sufficient investment into the inculcation of these beliefs to produce a high-trust society. Incredibly, this is true no matter how much parents care about their children.

Group Size and Trust

Travel anywhere and you will find plenty of trust behavior. Even in a low-trust society there is still a great deal of trust behavior due in large part to the power of harm-based moral restraint. The problem is that this is mostly small-group trust. So in every society most people trust family members, friends, and neighbors. They also trust those with whom they repeatedly interact. But in low-trust societies they are suspicious of strangers even in their own society, even those who practice the same religion with great zeal. And they certainly don't trust most organizations or governments.

Small-group trust works through mechanisms that require knowledge of others if they are to be trusted, so small-group trust simply does not work with total strangers. This is why it is often said that trust must be earned. In low-trust societies what looks like trust is not genuine trust but assurance that strangers won't take advantage of us in a given circumstance because it is impossible for them to do so or because it is not in their best interest to do so.

Some of our innate traits that support small-group trust work against large-group trust. If we can only trust those who are known to us either because we know they care about us or because they have earned our trust, then we will not trust those unknown to us. This limits trust to groups within which we know everyone well, making those living in other groups better targets for opportunism than for cooperation. It leads to "us" versus "them" thinking that is the essence of tribalism. The high-trust society is therefore a bulwark against tribalism because when strangers can trust each other in most circumstances, tribalism becomes costly and therefore foolish.

Trust and Development

The high-trust society has two forms of large-group trust. The first form is *generalized bilateral trust*, which refers to extending trust to individuals and organizations (including strangers) in most circumstances. The more extensive is this convention, the more accurate it is to describe a society as being a high-trust society. The second form is *trust in the system*, which refers to having confidence that those who have the power to change the rules that govern society will not do so for arbitrary or self-serving reasons. The more trust there is in the system, the more accurate it is to describe a society as being a high-trust society.

Most trust research pertains to bilateral trust in small-group contexts. Some involves bilateral trust across entire societies (generalized bilateral trust).[1] But almost no work has addressed the concept of trust in the system.[2] This chapter will focus on the rise of generalized bilateral trust. Although the arguments made in this chapter pertain to trust in the system, trust in the system will be discussed fully in the next chapter.

Generalized Bilateral Trust

Generalized bilateral trust is the widespread practice of rationally extending trust to other individuals and organizations that are presumed to be trustworthy. It requires that people trust each other in large-group contexts. It also requires that people trust strangers, so it is the very antithesis of earned trust. These two requirements leave out an important detail.

It is easy to imagine that one is willing to trust complete strangers with some kinds of transactions (holding your place in line at a fast-food restaurant) but not others (watching over a large bag of cash). This means that presuming strangers can be trusted is conditional on the circumstances involved. Circumstances that involve greater potential risk to the trusting individual require higher levels of trust. In other words, even in a high-trust society some transactions require a measure of earned trust.

At the same time, trustworthiness is not absolute, because it is produced through expected feelings of guilt and expected feelings of guilt are a matter of degree. So while one way to think of economic development is as an increase in the size of the groups over which trust can be presumed for a given type of transaction, another way to think of economic development is as an increase in the set of transaction types for which it is rational to presumptively extend trust in a society that is already large enough to produce mass flourishing.

Societies enjoy low transaction costs when individuals and organizations can rationally presume trustworthiness on the part of others. But the word "generalized" in "generalized bilateral trust" means that it applies in presumptive fashion to people in general. It does not mean that it applies to transactions in general. Generalized bilateral trust is implicitly conditioned on the type of transaction. Even in a very low-trust society there is generalized bilateral trust with respect to many transactions. But even in a very high-trust society banks store cash in vaults.

Let us define a set of transactions as "viable" if a sufficiently high proportion of a society's population is *trustworthy enough* for it to be rational to presume anyone else can be trusted with respect to those transactions. This requires a critical mass of individuals to have been taught trust-producing moral beliefs at an early age so as to create a prevailing ethic of duty-based moral restraint. The greater is the average level of duty-based moral restraint, the guiltier people will, on average, expect to feel if they behave opportunistically. This increases the set of transactions over which it is rational to presume that others, even strangers, can be trusted. Put another way, the greater is the average level of duty-based moral restraint, the smaller will be the set of transactions that require a measure of earned trust.

The Ladder of Development

Jeffrey Sachs famously invoked the metaphor of a ladder of economic development in his book *The End of Poverty* (2005). Sachs argued that humans are naturally good at market economic activity, so the real problem is to get the process started. This is because once growth gets going, positive feedback effects inevitably push societies to ever higher levels of development. The key is getting up the first few rungs.

I shall now argue that in reality, the farther up the ladder a society climbs the harder it becomes to keep climbing. This is because as society grows and prospers, there are increasingly strong incentives against adequate investment in trust-producing moral beliefs. So the rise of truly flourishing societies is like overcoming the problem of Sisyphus pushing a boulder up a hill except that the hill gets steeper as he goes. The higher he goes, the harder it is to climb further and the more likely the boulder will come rolling back down.

Many countries have reached respectable levels of development without being high-trust societies by relying on formal institutions to keep transaction costs reasonably low. This is no small achievement because it has alleviated a great deal of human misery. But the problem with this approach is that as economic activity is conducted in ever larger groups, institutions become increasingly unable to overcome the problem of opportunism without relying on strict procedures and routines. This undermines entrepreneurial culture that encourages creative problem-solving to adapt to changing conditions and to take advantage of new opportunities to create wealth.

Using institutions to provide assurance as a substitute for trust therefore produces a trade-off between group size and entrepreneurship. This trade-off is an obstacle to mass flourishing. We have had large-group cooperation for a long time, and we have had entrepreneurial behavior for a long time, but we have only had large-group cooperation directed in an entrepreneurial fashion (not just from the top but throughout) for a short time. We have also only had societies that produce mass flourishing for a short period of time.

Now consider a different kind of ladder of development that allows a society to climb to higher levels of cooperative activity and therefore to be able to support higher levels of flourishing. Lower steps are associated with transactions that require little trust. Each step up includes all of the transactions in the previous step plus additional ones that require additional trust. By climbing the ladder, a society can enjoy the benefits of presumptive extension of trust over ever larger sets of transactions through which the gains from cooperation can be realized.

This happens in a direct way because transaction costs are lower when dealing with trustworthy persons. But it also happens in an indirect way because as trust becomes more widespread in a society, additional trust-dependent institutions become viable that further reduce transaction costs and, hence, further increase the set of viable transactions. For both reasons, climbing the ladder increases the gains from cooperation, which increases output per person, which is the first step to driving up general prosperity to increase mass flourishing.

Increasing duty-based moral restraint for a given proportion of the population or increasing the proportion of the population that abides by a given level of duty-based moral restraint increases the set of viable transactions. As a general matter, more investment into the inculcation of trust-producing moral beliefs across society increases the size of the viable transaction set, which lets a society climb further up the ladder.

The Cultural Commons Dilemma Revisited

Recall that the cultural commons is subject to the problems of abuse and neglect. Climbing the ladder of development can be thought of as doing an ever better job addressing the abuse problem. By making an ethic of duty-based moral restraint stronger and more widespread, the abuse problem can be reduced.

Consider this extreme example. Suppose everyone in a society is taught moral beliefs that produce an ethic of duty-based moral restraint. Suppose they are taught these beliefs so early in life that such beliefs work through tastes that function prerationally. Suppose they are taught these beliefs so strongly that expected feelings guilt are so high that everyone can be trusted with respect to all transactions. In this case a perfectly high-trust society will result.

Getting closer to this ideal requires getting ever better at solving the neglect problem. But this is not in reference to the neglect problem associated with inadequate investment in prosocial behaviors and moral values. It is in reference to the neglect problem associated with inadequate investment in duty-based moral restraint to combat the abuse problem.

Put directly, the *primary* neglect problem is failing to invest enough resources in period t to produce a sufficiently strong and widespread ethic of duty-based moral restraint in period $t + 1$ so as to adequately address the abuse problem in period $t + 1$. Such a solution pertains to a given step on the ladder of development. The adequate level of investment rises with each step up on the ladder. So solving the primary neglect problem ever better is the key to increasingly unleashing the power of cooperation by climbing the ladder of development. But the primary neglect problem is a very difficult problem to solve.

The Public Good Problem

One reason why high-trust societies are rare is that the kind of moral beliefs required to produce duty-based moral restraint are not grounded in our innate moral intuitions. But making matters far worse is that such trust-producing moral beliefs also have qualities that produce a public good problem that drives a wedge between the level of investment that parents are likely to choose and the level of investment that best promotes the common good.

For a society to be a high-trust society, it is not enough for the adults of period t to know, understand, and endorse trust-producing moral beliefs and therefore share them with their children. Teaching trust-producing moral beliefs as early and as widely as possible is necessary but not sufficient because there is also the issue of moral conviction, which is derived from the strength of moral tastes. The stronger are trust-producing moral tastes, the guiltier an individual will expect to feel if he behaves opportunistically, and so the larger will be the set of transactions over which he will refrain from opportunism and therefore behave in trustworthy manner.

Transmitting moral beliefs is costly. This is especially true for the kind of moral beliefs that support large-group trust because they are abstract and do not benefit from being rooted in our small-group moral intuitions. At the same time, the primary beneficiaries of such investment are not the ones making the investment, but the adults of the next generation. Such investment is therefore largely a sacrifice of one generation's resources for the next generation's benefit.

This is not necessarily an insurmountable problem. One can imagine that most parents are willing to sacrifice a great amount of their own resources because they love their children and are therefore made happy by knowing they are helping them grow up to be happy. So as long as most parents care greatly about their children's future, it would seem that the fact that the inculcation of the required moral beliefs is costly is not necessarily problematic.

But even if every parent cares more about his children than himself, parents are still not likely to invest enough resources to produce a high-trust society. The problem is that, to the extent that the beliefs involved are able to produce a high-trust society, they are effectively social human capital that constitutes a public good.

Social Capital

Human capital refers to traits possessed by individuals that can be used to promote that individual's welfare.[3] Traits that support trustworthiness therefore benefit individuals because other people prefer transacting with trustworthy individuals. Trust-producing moral beliefs are therefore a form of human capital.

But moral beliefs that produce trustworthy individuals benefit other individuals, too, because those other individuals won't be cheated. Those who live in societies dominated by such individuals also benefit from the existence of trust-dependent institutions that further lower transaction costs.

Because of this, trust-producing moral beliefs are more than human capital, they are also *social* capital. This is because the social gains arising from such beliefs exceed the private gains.[4] Unfortunately, this presents parents with the worry that if other parents don't make such investments, they and their children will be making sacrifices to sustain the high-trust society while other parents don't. The children of these other parents can benefit from behaving opportunistically, possibly at their own children's expense. This is an example of what game theorists call the "sucker's payoff." I will return to this important issue in chapters 7 and 8.

Moreover, the same attributes that make trust-producing moral beliefs social capital also make them public goods. This is a problem because public goods are not naturally provided in sufficient measure to best promote the common good. This is because with public goods, two things drive a wedge between private action and what is best for the common good. They are nonrival consumption and nonexcludable consumption.

Non-rival Consumption

A person whose trustworthiness is derived from moral tastes doesn't become less trustworthy to me because he was trustworthy to someone else. So those who benefit from transacting with a trustworthy person are engaging in what economists call nonrival consumption. The benefits arising from a high-trust society are largely nonrival in nature. This is true for two reasons.

First, being trustworthy doesn't require action—it requires not acting in an untrustworthy way. Therefore, Bob can be trustworthy toward everyone. Sue doesn't use up Bob's trustworthiness when she trusts him the way she would use up Bob's hamburger if she ate it. Benefiting from another individuals' trustworthiness is therefore nonrival.

Second, in a high-trust society individuals and organizations are able to do things more easily because trust-dependent institutions can exist. Bob's benefiting from the existence of a given trust-dependent institution does not undermine Sue's ability to benefit from it, too. Benefiting from the existence of a trust-dependent institution is also, to some extent anyway, nonrival.[5]

Nonexcludable Consumption

Virtually every person who transacts with a trustworthy individual benefits from that individual's trustworthiness. This produces a premium for trustworthy individuals if they can signal their trustworthiness and exclude those who are unwilling to pay a premium for having benefited from it. In other words, if you want an honest plumber you'll have to pay for an honest plumber. So if Sue is trustworthy, her ability to refuse to transact with Bob gives her the ability to force him to pay a premium for some of the benefit that her trustworthiness creates for him. The expected benefits to Sue arising from such excludable trustworthiness would have given Sue's parents an incentive to make her trustworthy.

This is the natural way for a rational choice theorist to think of the investment problem, as a problem of human capital investment that largely solves itself from incentives arising from expected future benefits. But this does not account for the fact that much of the benefit of living in a high-trust society is nonexcludable. Even a very untrustworthy person lives a much better life in a high-trust society than in a low-trust one. These benefits cannot be withheld because they are nonexcludable, so the payment of a premium cannot be compelled by any individual. So to the extent that trust-producing moral beliefs produce nonexcludable benefits from a high-trust society, there are no private incentives for their investment.

In a society in which nearly everyone expects to experience a great deal of guilt when behaving in an untrustworthy way, the set of transactions over which it is rational to presume others can be trusted is quite large. How guilty an individual expects to feel when behaving in an untrustworthy way is affected by many things. Adults whose parents invested a great deal of resources into the inculcation of trust-producing moral beliefs will, on average, feel guiltier than adults who had parents who invested little.

If the rational promotion of one's own child's material welfare is all that determines the level of investment, parents will simply compare the private costs and private benefits involved. The private benefit is the utility parents derive from increasing the likelihood their children will prosper because they will be trustworthy adults. The private cost is the time and money spent teaching, monitoring, and meting out punishments and rewards.

This *privately rational* level of investment selected by parents varies from family to family, but whatever the resulting level of investment turns out to be for each family, it produces a convention of presumptively extending trust over a set of transactions of particular size. Let's call this set of viable transactions T_0. But had all parents invested a little more, their children would, on average, experience a little more guilt upon behaving opportunistically. This would have increased the set of viable transactions, which would have allowed more cooperation to occur, which would increase the value of output per person.

How Nonexcludability Impedes
Large-Group Trust

Incredibly, even if the increase in the value of output per future adult rises by far more than the additional cost of investment per future adult to bring about that result, such investment is not likely to happen in a large society. Suppose there are always 1,000 adults in a society. Suppose that when parents in period t invest the privately rational level of effort into inculcating trust-producing moral beliefs, the set of viable transactions that results, T_0, supports enough cooperation to produce $5,000 worth of total output. This produces an average payoff of $5 of output per adult in period $t + 1$.

Now suppose that if parents in period t had invested $3 more of resources into the inculcation of trust-producing moral beliefs, the typical adult in $t + 1$ could be trusted to engage in more tempting types of transactions and more trust-dependent institutions could exist. Suppose that this increases the set of viable transactions to $T_1 > T_0$.

The sum of the value of the cooperative surpluses for viable transaction set of T_1 is higher than for T_0, which increases the value of total output for society even though the population is the same. At the same time, the society enjoys a windfall in the form of being able to consume resources that would have otherwise gone toward safeguarding against opportunistic behavior. Suppose that because of all of these gains, the value of output increases to $100,000, thereby increasing the average payoff to $100 per person.[6]

So $3 of additional moral training increases the average payoff by $95. If parents care as much about their children as they do about themselves, this is a very good deal. But there is a problem. The larger the society is, the truer it is that the actions of any single individual will not overturn the convention of presumptively extending trust over any given set of viable transactions and therefore will not result in stepping down the ladder of development.

At the same time, many of the benefits of living in a higher-trust society are non-excludable, so they can be enjoyed by individuals whose parents did not invest the additional $3 of resources into moral training. There is therefore no way to force parents to pay for the higher quality of life their children will enjoy by living in a higher-trust society that can support the $T_1 > T_0$ set of transactions in period $t + 1$.

Since the children of parents who did not invest the additional $3 also get to enjoy many of these benefits, parents have no incentive to invest the extra $3 of resources because their *private* investment decision will not change the *social* outcome. A higher-trust society will or will not happen regardless of what they do, so they can only change the outcome for their own child. They therefore invest an amount that is best for themselves and their children, not an amount that best promotes the common good. There is no point in investing more. Doing so would be irrational.

Note that this result isn't changed by increasing how much parents care about their children or how much they care about society as a whole because they are unable to affect the level of social trust. Indeed, we will see later that increasing how much they care about their children can actually reduce the likelihood of the existence of a high-trust society.[7]

Unfortunately, these incentives are the same for everyone in this example, so none of the parents spends the extra $3, the set of transactions does not grow, and the increase in the value of output per person does not rise by $95. The result is demonstrably worse for the common good. Even if everyone understands this, they know they are powerless to change the outcome. All they can do is invest the extra $3 to no avail. Because they cannot bring about a higher-trust society through their own actions, they know they will help their children more by simply giving them the $3 or putting it toward better food, healthcare, schooling, violin lessons, and so forth.

This brings us to an important observation. When the level of investment in trust-producing moral beliefs rises to levels that begin producing a high-trust society—a society with trust-dependent institutions like presumptively extending trust and honest judicial systems—such moral beliefs increasingly cross over from being merely human capital to also being social capital. Since the same attributes that make such human capital also social capital fulfill the definition of public good, this can also be thought of as increasingly crossing over from their being private goods to their being public goods.

Up the Ladder of Development

From the new state (T_1) we can consider what would happen if yet another $3 is invested per in each child of generation t. This additional investment would drive expected guilt costs higher and therefore expand the set of viable transactions to $T_2 > T_1$. Yet more investment would have the same effect ($T_3 > T_2 > T_1$). Each increase in the size of the viable set of transactions would then produce additional increases in the value of output per person.

Increasing the size of the set of viable transaction step by step is how a society climbs up the ladder of development. More investment increases the size of the viable transaction set and therefore leads to more cooperation by extending the reach of the presumptive trust. Some of the institutions that rightfully get credit for making the climb are themselves largely byproducts of the very high levels of trust made possible by climbing the ladder well up from the ground because they are, themselves, trust dependent.

In his highly influential book *The Mystery of Capital* (2000), Hernando de Soto argued that capitalism triumphed in the West because of strong property rights institutions. This allowed for the accumulation of capital in private hands, where it was entrepreneurially employed. But why weren't strong property rights institutions adopted elsewhere? Perhaps they weren't because property rights institutions are themselves trust dependent. It does little good to register property with a government office that might use such information to cheat the landowner.

This analysis does not imply that it is possible or even desirable for societies to become perfectly high-trust societies. As a society climbs the ladder of development, eventually additional gains will become smaller. After 99.9% of all people can be completely trusted with 99.9% of all transactions, for example, there is not much additional gain to be had. Long before this point, the additional gains will almost certainly become too small to cover the additional cost. In short, the benefits of a perfectly high-trust society are not worth the cost of achieving it.

Three Development Milestones

Relational Contracts

Recall that relational contracts allow those who possess local knowledge the discretion to act on it. Relational contracts therefore increase organizational efficiency by speeding up adaptation to changing conditions. But relational contracts are a highly trust-dependent institution. So in low-trust societies, relational contracts can only be used with people who are well known.

The inability to use relational contracts in widespread fashion is why in low-trust societies so much large-scale cooperative activity is coordinated in a bureaucratic rather than entrepreneurial fashion. In low-trust societies, entrepreneurial decision-making is necessarily limited to small enterprises because relational contracts cannot be used in large-group contexts. As noted earlier, this creates a trade-off between size and entrepreneurship that is an obstacle to development.

As a society climbs the ladder of development, larger sets of transactions fall under presumptive trust. This means there is an increasing number of decision-makers who can be trusted with discretion. This increases the amount of economic activity that can be coordinated in an entrepreneurial fashion even in large-group contexts.

Collective Creativity

The key to improving the quality of life continuously over time is continuously improving productivity. Robert Solow, who won the

Nobel Prize in Economics in 1987 for his work on economic growth, demonstrated over a half-century ago that to increase the value of output per person, something more than reinvesting into the capital stock was required.[8] Solow argued that, for capital of a given type, adding more without adding more labor eventually produces ever smaller gains. At some point the growing cost of maintaining the capital stock begins to exceed the gains in output, so growth through "capital deepening" ends.

If, however, an innovation can produce a new kind of capital that is more productive, then the story changes. Of particular importance are innovations like the steam engine or silicon chips that improve productivity over much of society. Such dramatic innovations are more likely to occur in societies that support collective creativity. Every society has its share of creative geniuses, but even an exceptional brain can only do so much. To unlock the full potential of human creativity, many people have to work together.

Employees and managers will be creative only to the extent that they can trust those they work with, their immediate supervisors, and the owners of the firm. This is because it is very difficult to protect cocreator interests through formal contracts since the course of creative activity cannot be predicted. Individuals and organizations must also be able to trust that the rewards from their creative efforts will not be rendered moot by corporate or government power (e.g., arbitrary changes to compensation policies or to tax rates).

Collective Science

Hyperspecialization is the hallmark of modern science because the breadth of scientific knowledge is too great to make progress in any other way. But this means that scientists must have a great deal of trust in the scientific research of other scientists. Otherwise they will be reluctant to use the work of other scientists to advance their respective fields.

This is one of the most important reasons why trust is so important for supporting human flourishing and advancement.

Basic scientific research is what ultimately produces most of the discoveries that produce the largest payoffs to society. But if scientists cannot trust the work of other scientists, scientific progress slows to a crawl because it is simply too hard to know more than a small part of any given field.

Addressing the Public Good Problem

There is a strong bias against sufficient investment in trust-producing moral beliefs to produce a high-trust society. As Matt Ridley (1997) powerfully argues, the spread of trade no doubt helped spread trade supporting virtues that civilized us in far reaching ways. But it does not follow from this argument that the level of investment that best promotes the common good will be undertaken. This means we should be skeptical of hopeful accounts in which some market activity increases returns to honesty, and this, in turn, increases investment in moral training that leads to even more market activity, and so on. Long before a level of investment required to best promote the common good is achieved, the additional private returns to further investment won't cover the additional private costs of achieving it. Parents will find that it is better to simply give these resources to their children or to invest them into their children's human capital in other ways.

It follows that for a society to enjoy increasing flourishing, more is required than simply stumbling upon trust-producing moral beliefs and teaching them to the next generation. There is at least one additional necessary condition: addressing this public good problem. The more fully the public good problem is addressed, the more a society can flourish. Solving public good problems is one of the strongest arguments for having government. Is there a way to use government to address this particular public good problem? In the next chapter we will see why using government—especially democratic government—to address this public good problem is not likely to work.

But there is another way to address the problem and, remarkably, it is through culture itself. In short, cultural content in the form of certain kinds of nonmoral beliefs might complement moral beliefs in ways that drive up investment. I address the nature of such beliefs in chapter 8. The more fully such beliefs complement trust-producing moral beliefs per se, the more human capital in the form of previously learned trust-producing moral beliefs goes beyond helping the individual succeed, functioning as social capital that benefits everyone.

Notes

1. The most famous example is the World Values Survey question that asks, "Generally speaking, would you say that most people can be trusted or that you can't be too careful in dealing with people?"

2. An exception to this rule is a report from the Regulatory Policy Institute (2009) titled *Trust in the System*.

3. Gary Becker (1964) is considered the seminal contribution to human capital theory which has proven to be an enormously rich concept.

4. James Coleman and Robert Putnam are credited with the most important early work on social capital. See Sobel (2002), Ostrom and Ahn (2003), Durlauf and Fafchamps (2006), and Guiso et al. (2008) for excellent reviews of this literature. Glaeser et. al. (2002) first introduced the concept of individual social capital, which I call *social human capital*.

5. Even if never actually used, an honest judicial system allows Bob to use formal contracts with strangers to coordinate business activity to do things more efficiently.

6. A comparison of GDP per person in high-trust societies relative to low-trust societies shows that this is far from unrealistic (see, for example, Knack and Keefer 1997; Knack and Zak 2001).

7. This chapter fixes the content of moral beliefs to focus on the public good problem. We will see in chapter 7 how this can also result in changes to moral beliefs that undermine trust.

8. Solow's work is extensive and continues to influence work in economic growth. His most famous paper, "A Contribution to the Theory of Economic Growth," was written in 1956.

PART II

IMPLICATIONS FOR FREE MARKET DEMOCRACY

6

The Free Market Democracy Dilemma

Even in a high-trust society there will be some untrustworthy people. Since even a small proportion of untrustworthy people can dramatically drive up transaction costs, there is a need for a government with police powers. But, unfortunately, one of the oldest and truest saws in political economy is that a government powerful enough to fight crime, enforce contracts, and enforce property rights is also powerful enough to coerce its citizens.[1]

Since government is capable of doing tremendous harm, mass flourishing requires that we be able to trust that government power will be used only to advance the common good. Using government power to coerce citizens *beyond* enforcing the rules that citizens have freely agreed to live by is not consistent with freedom. Democracy provides a check on government power by giving citizens the ability to remove from power those who abuse the power entrusted to them.

In the absence of democracy, those in control of government must pull together support from elite groups to produce coalitions of support. To garner such support, power is required to extract resources from society to be used to reward supporters. This leaves fewer resources to pay for public goods that increase the common good. Such redistribution makes enemies as well as friends. Dictators therefore try to minimize the size of the coalition needed to hold onto power lest they engender widespread revolt.[2] In principle, then, democracy can help a society use government power toward the provision of genuine public goods that advance the common good rather than the provision of private goods that only secure continued political support.

Free market systems and democracies operate through well-known institutions. Many of these institutions ultimately rest on a cultural foundation because they depend on the existence of a high-trust society made possible by culture. One reason why culture is so important is precisely because institutions are so important, but many of them are highly trust dependent.

There are many well-known arguments for why capitalism and freedom are mutually reinforcing.[3] The existence of the mutually reinforcing effects of capitalism and freedom are indicated in our diagram of how culture ultimately supports mass flourishing with a double arrowed line in figure 6.1. We now turn to the task of explaining how the free market system and democracy can also be self-defeating.

Trust in the System

Trust in the system is having confidence that those who have the power to change the rules that govern society will not do so for arbitrary or self-serving reasons. No matter how low transactions costs are between transacting individuals or organizations, incentives for socially beneficial cooperation can still be negated by those who have power over the system. For a society to enjoy mass flourishing, people must also believe that rules are reasonably stable as well as competently and fairly enforced.

Suppose two people can work together to produce a cooperative surplus. Suppose each trusts the other completely. If either thinks that those who have the power to change the rules of society are likely to change them in a way that wipes out the value of the surplus, then cooperation will not occur. Conversely, when people have trust in the system they are confident that their time, effort, and investments are not going to become the spoils of those who have power over the rules that govern the system.

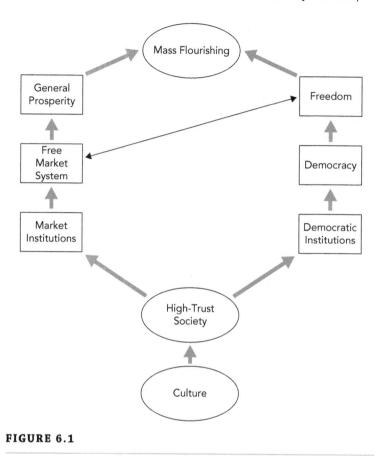

FIGURE 6.1

The mutually reinforcing nature of capitalism and freedom

The greater is generalized bilateral trust and the greater is trust in the system, the more accurately a given society can be described as being a high-trust society. Trust in each other keeps the expected cost of transacting low, while trust in the system keeps the expected net gain from transacting high. This maximizes the scale and scope of transactions, which is the key to maximizing mass flourishing.

Trust in the system becomes more important as groups grow in size. Trust in the system is largely built on government institutions that are very costly for any society. To maintain trust in the system government must, for example, be able to enforce criminal law, enforce contracts, and enforce property rights. These activities normally have a high ratio of fixed to variable costs, so the key to having them is having a large number of transactions over which to spread such costs.

There is great potential for large-group cooperation facilitated by government mechanisms that only large societies can afford, but these mechanisms can be subverted by those in power. No matter how productive any society is, government can destroy incentives so thoroughly that it impoverishes the society. The rise of flourishing societies is therefore as much a story of the rise of good government that produces trust in the system as it is a story of the rise of generalized bilateral trust and increasingly complex institutions.

At some level nearly everyone understands that a flourishing society requires trust in the system and that good government is required for such trust to exist. But since most trust research focuses on bilateral trust, the role that trust in the system might play in supporting the development and operation of free market democracies has received little attention.[4] So while most people already believe trust in the system is important, we actually know very little about it.

Free Market Institutions

Contracts

Virtually all societies can sustain commercial behavior in the form of simple spot market transactions (e.g., street vendors who sell food for cash), but many transactions must be coordinated by contracts. The ability to create and enforce contracts has allowed some societies to dramatically increase the set of viable transactions, and therefore the scale and scope of cooperation. But for contracts to work well, they must be enforceable at relatively low cost.

Societies that have developed a clear and consistent body of contract law and a competent judiciary that can be trusted to be impartial are able to use contracts to engage in significantly more complex transactions than societies that have not. Every additional transaction made possible by such enhanced contracting ability is another source of cooperative surplus that adds to general prosperity and is ultimately dependent on trust in the system.

Private Property Rights

People can think ahead. So the more likely that gains from transacting can be taken later by those with power, the more people will discount such gains. This reduces the incentive to engage in transactions, which reduces the value of output per person in a society.

If those who possess the power to take one's property choose to use that power to honestly enforce private property rights, then the expected return from transacting is increased. The more confidence there is that property rights will be competently and impartially enforced, the stronger will be incentives to engage in industrious behavior. This behavior requires laws and policies that respect property rights, and it requires the honest enforcement of those laws and policies. To have trust in the system, one must have confidence these requirements will be met.

Sound Money

It is hard to imagine anything in the development of market economic systems that did more to reduce transaction costs than the emergence of money. An extensive literature explains why.[5] Money dramatically increases economic efficiency. But when its value changes unpredictably it can cause tremendous upheavals in societies. Milton Friedman is famous for saying, "There is nothing which will destroy a society so thoroughly and so fully as letting inflation run riot."[6]

People who lend money to entrepreneurs can be wiped out by un-expected inflation, so when there is fear that the value of money will not be preserved, far less is loaned, and that which is loaned is loaned at a higher rate of interest. This reduces the ability of entrepreneurs to invest in activities that ultimately promote the common good. At the same time, fear of deflation can discourage borrowing to pay for capital that ultimately promotes the common good since debt payments remain constant but income out of which to pay them falls.

There has been nearly endless debate over the virtues of fiat money versus commodity monies like gold or silver. Virtually everyone agrees that if a society has a fiat form of money, then government must be trusted not to abuse its ability to alter the value of money for politically expedient purposes. Sound money is crucial for producing mass flourishing, but with fiat money this soundness depends on a government that can be trusted to maintain its value.

This steadiness is much harder than it sounds. Monetary authorities must not waver when political pressure is put on them to pursue politically expedient policies. Among other things, this requires that political leaders refrain from engaging in deficit spending that increases pressure on monetary authorities to monetize debt. All of this is required for there to be sound money, which, in turn, is required for there to be trust in the system.

Democratic Institutions

Democracy is valuable because it provides checks on government power. But for this counterbalance to work, citizens must believe that voting is honestly conducted. Only then will they accept the outcome when it doesn't go their way. Even a small amount of distrust of the voting system can therefore lead to serious problems. Trust in the system therefore requires honestly run elections.

The Media

The corporate firm governance structure requires a great deal of transparency if it is to best promote the common good. People are most willing to buy a corporation's shares if they are confident that nothing illegal or unethical is afoot. Unfortunately, a diligent Securities and Exchange Commission can only provide so much assurance. Rule-driven bureaucracies produce fixed targets for the likes of Enron and WorldCom to circumvent.

The media are therefore very important for having trust in the system. Evading investigative reporters is much harder than gaming bureaucratic rules. Honestly run corporate firms benefit from a diligent and trustworthy media because potential share buyers will have greater faith that the information the firm provides about itself is accurate.[7] The less confidence the public has in the competency, diligence, and honesty of the media, the less confidence the public will have in the free market system.

Constitutional democracies can evolve into very large and complex governments. Ordinary voters therefore depend heavily on a determined press to chase down impropriety. So the less confidence the public has in the integrity of the media, the less confidence the public will have in the democratic system. Distrust in the media contributes to the belief that no one can trust the society's institutions, which also undermines trust in the system.

There is ample evidence that trust in the media has fallen in recent years in the West and particularly in the United States. A recent large sample Gallup poll shows, for example, that the percentage of respondents who had a great to fair amount of trust in the mass media fell from 53% in 1997 to 32% in 2016. Even more disturbing was that trust in the mass media from 2001 to 2016 fell twice as fast for adults 18–49 (−29%) as for adults 50 and older (−12%).[8]

Trust in the System as a Substitute for Generalized Bilateral Trust

Governments that wish to foster rapid economic growth in societies with low generalized bilateral trust know they have little ability to quickly change the level of trust that citizens have in each other. But such governments do have the ability to act in other ways that signal they understand the importance of strong incentives. Governments can strive to produce trust in the system to substitute for the lack of generalized bilateral trust.

In many societies people look to government to provide order by smoothing over tribal differences between groups. This can produce a measure of trust in the system that reduces transaction costs and produces a measure of social harmony. In Yugoslavia, for example, ethnic animosities had been suppressed by government. This facilitated a modest level of economic activity, but once Yugoslavia dissolved into separate republics, it became clear that trust in the system provided by the central government was substituting for, rather than contributing to, generalized bilateral trust.

Singapore provides another example of how a heterogeneous population (there are four official languages) comprising many groups that rank low on the World Values Trust Survey can nevertheless conduct commercial activity because of strong trust in the system. As of the last census taken in 2010, over 90% of Singapore's residents owned their own homes. At the same time, Singapore is an economic powerhouse. What is its secret?

Singapore inherited strong commercial and legal institutions from Britain and, although its democracy is not without flaws and its early government was not without corruption, trust in the system to enforce contracts and property rights was nevertheless very high due in large part to the strong leadership by Lee Kuan Yew.[9] Lee Kuan Yew's faith in the free market system was widely regarded as sincere, and those who decided that Singapore's government institutions could be trusted were quickly proven correct. This led to increasing trust in the system and helps explain why in 2015 Singapore was ranked as the second freest economy in the world in the Index of Economic Freedom prepared by the Heritage Foundation and the *Wall Street Journal*.

Development

American history is rich with scoundrels. There has been no shortage of con artists, snake oil salesman, carpetbaggers, unscrupulous tycoons, crooked politicians, and so forth. Americans trusted their families, friends, fellow churchgoers, and neighbors, but there is no evidence that they trusted complete strangers to any greater degree than other societies. Movies about the American West often portrayed heroes whose word was their bond. But audiences understood this to be an ideal for behavior, not a reflection of the norm of behavior. The hero was a hero precisely because he was exceptional.

Until the middle of the 20th century, most large cities in America remained highly segregated into neighborhoods that were often very tribal in nature (consider the warring gangs in the musical *West Side Story*). But while there was not much personal trust outside of these groups, there was still a great deal of trust in the system compared to the countries that most people had emigrated from. This was due in part to a constitutional government designed to diffuse power.

From the beginning Americans did not put a great deal of trust in most of their political leaders. They thought that most politicians were scoundrels who were out for themselves. But America was bigger than its leaders. By having a system that was good at limiting the power of its political leaders, America engendered strong trust in the system.

So for most of America's history trust in the system was very high. The possibility that one could become rich only to have the government take the money later was unfathomable. Most ordinary people did not become rich, but many saw other ordinary people become rich. They also saw that the government did not then take their property.

The Logic of Collective Action

We tend to think of democracy as an invention of the modern world, beginning with the ancient Greeks. But it is more likely that primitive forms of democracy were practiced much earlier, while we still lived exclusively in small groups. Mancur Olson (1993) noted that both Tacitus and Caesar had observed that the Germanic tribes practiced an informal kind of voting that was so democratic that many did not have a chief.[10]

Christopher Boehm has argued that the roots of government began long ago with nonbullies ganging up on bullies. Democratic decision-making is a natural byproduct of this phenomenon.[11] It is therefore only natural that our small-group moral intuitions comport well with democracy, which may explain why democracy seems, to most people, to be self-evidently fair. But this also means that there is no particular reason why democracy should work well in large groups.

Greece gets all of the attention because it was the first instance for which we have written historical records of democracy being practiced in large groups. But it is instructive to note that democracy did not last in ancient Greece. Moreover, going back at least as far as Plato scholars have warned of the problems of democracy as a collective choice mechanism. Even by the time of Socrates, democracy was already showing signs of being maladapted to large-group contexts.

Greek concerns about democracy were not limited to fear of tyranny by the majority through an unsophisticated mob. Athenians were also worried about sophisticated individuals and interest groups manipulating the system for their own benefit. They became so worried about democracy being subverted by members of the elite bent on creating a ruling oligarchy that for a time they even adopted the practice of drawing lots to determine who would be chosen for public service.

It makes perfect sense that the first recorded warnings about democracy came from the ancient Greeks since they were the first to practice democracy on a large scale. Since then, other warnings have been issued about democracy by some of history's greatest thinkers, but all of these warnings are implicitly directed to democratic government—large-group rather than small-group collective decision-making.[12]

A common view today is to concede that democracy is necessary to provide a check on government power, but to then argue that because it can also lead to tyranny by the majority so it should be constrained through mechanisms like constitutions. But in one of the most influential books ever written about political economy, *The Logic of Collective Action* (1965), Mancur Olson explained why quite the opposite problem is likely to emerge.

Olson argued that when a special interest group is small relative to a society, it can vote in policies that benefit its members a great deal at the expense of society as a whole. Moreover, the larger a society becomes, the stronger will be incentives for special interest groups to use the democratic process to benefit themselves at the expense of the common good.[13]

Suppose there are 100,000 people in a society, 10 of whom are dairy farmers. Suppose the price of a gallon of milk is one dollar, everyone drinks one gallon of milk per week, and everyone earns $20,000 per year. If dairy farmers can get a law passed to raise the price of milk by five cents per gallon and the consumption of milk does not fall, this would more than double each dairy farmer's income, increasing it to $46,000 per year. But this tremendous benefit to dairy farmers only increases everyone's yearly milk bill by $2.60, which is less than 0.013% of their income. Olson's point was that the smaller a special interest group is relative to society, the greater the divergence between the net gains to those in the special interest group and the costs borne by everyone else.

Redistributive and Regulatory Favoritism

The dairy farmer example above reflects *redistributive favoritism* because it involves a law or policy that favors a specific group by redistributing resources from society to members of that group. Many laws and policies, however, involve some measure of redistribution but are not examples of redistributive favoritism because the redistribution involved promotes the common good.[14] But even these laws and policies are often implemented beyond a level that best promotes the common good because of the interest group incentives discussed by Olson.

Regulatory favoritism refers to regulatory laws or policies that help one firm or one industry at the expense of society.

A well-known argument is that regulatory agencies can reduce economic efficiency by unwittingly facilitating tacit collusion between those who are to be regulated.[15] What starts out as a sincere attempt to protect consumers from powerful firms and industries becomes a mechanism for crony capitalism that undermines the common good.

Consider the airline industry in the United States before 1978. As air travel expanded, the federal government increasingly worried about air safety so it created the Civil Aeronautics Board in 1938. It expanded its regulatory powers in 1958 by creating the Federal Aviation Administration (FAA). The goal was to keep planes from running into each other because too many of them were flying to the same place at the same time. Unfortunately, the power to limit flights to a safe level could be used to limit flights even further to reduce operating costs while driving up airfares.

The FAA's regulations thereby produced outcomes that would have almost certainly engendered prosecution from the Justice Department had the airlines privately achieved them among themselves. This is why when the airlines were deregulated in 1978 the industry was almost immediately transformed. The harm to society of regulatory favoritism was made evident by its removal through deregulation by the Carter administration, which quickly resulted in more flights and lower fares and air travel went from an elite activity to a common one.

The same problem makes both redistributive and regulatory favoritism socially harmful. While some measure of government involvement often promotes the common good, incentives to use the democratic process to promote special interests don't magically disappear once the level of redistribution or regulation that best promotes the common good is achieved.

A common objection to Olson's point is that while a given special interest group can benefit its members at the expense of society, anyone can form or join a special interest group and, in so doing, neutralize the harm done to them by also being on the receiving end of this game. Those who complain about this response are then portrayed as politically naive sore losers. In the end everyone, except the politically inept, should be able to use the system for their own benefit so everything evens out. I get mine, you get yours.

In his famous example of splitting a lunch bill evenly, Russell Roberts (1995) explained why this is simply not true. The larger a group is, the more likely it is that everyone will order the most expensive item because he is likely to end up paying for expensive items the other diners order. So to avoid being a chump, everyone eats an expensive meal, and the prophecy becomes self-fulfilling.

Even though superficially everyone gets his cut, as it were, this is still a bad outcome. Many in the group end up paying for the most expensive item which, for them, wasn't worth what they had to pay to get it. They would not have chosen it if they simply paid their own bill. But the larger the group, the truer it is that when any given individual refuses to order the most expensive thing, it saves him almost nothing because the bill is divided equally.

Olson's and Roberts's point is that while one small special interest group in a large society can benefit tremendously through political favoritism, it does not follow that everyone can join a special interest group to enjoy the fruits of favoritism in like measure. Redistributive and regulatory favoritism is more about individual groups benefiting at the expense of the common good than it is about dividing resources more wisely through political rather than economic mechanisms.

Clearly the best outcome for society is for no special interest group to exploit the democratic process to promote its members' welfare at the expense of the common good. The problem is that any individual special interest group does best when it exploits the democratic process while every other special interest group does not. This is just another case of individual rationality undermining the common good, but here "individual" pertains to individual special interest groups.

Unfortunately, as more special interest groups exploit the democratic process, the incentive for others to do so becomes even stronger. The only thing worse than playing a futile game is not doing so while others do! Special interest groups that do not attempt to exploit the democratic process end up getting none of the benefits of favoritism while bearing the cost. This is another example of what game theorists call the sucker's payoff.

So special interest groups that exploit the democratic process induce others to form such groups. This increasingly wipes out the gains that were so great when there were only a few small special interest groups, while making it increasingly imperative that individuals either form or join a special interest group.

Increasingly resources are spent in zero-sum special interest group competition for political favoritism. Many of these resources come from what would have otherwise been positive-sum cooperative activity. This means that an activity that, at best, leaves the value output unchanged also uses up resources that could have increased the value of output per person.

By reducing the size of the economic pie and distorting how it is divided, redistributive and regulatory favoritism reduces the return to productive activity and thereby engenders less of it. This further reduces the value of output. The adverse effect of redistributive and regulatory favoritism on incentives associated with cooperation is indicated by the dashed line in figure 6.2.

The Rule of Law

The rule of law requires that no one be above the law and that it be enforced without favoritism. It also requires that the law be interpreted in good faith. So when the letter of the law cannot be directly applied to a particular circumstance, those in regulatory agencies and in the judiciary must do their best to follow the spirit of the law by endeavoring to abide by the intent of the law *even if they do not personally approve of it.*

Those who have a pessimistic view of government are quick to spot problems of governmental favoritism. But those who have an optimistic view of government should also be concerned about favoritism. The more one understands how important government is for supporting cooperation that best promotes the common

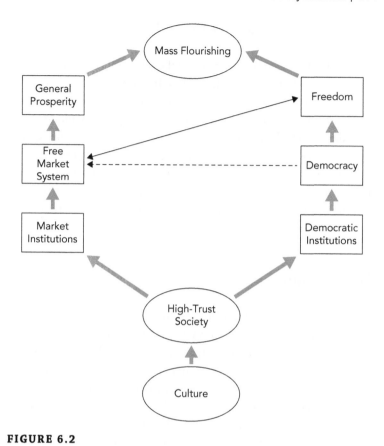

FIGURE 6.2

Adverse effects of redistributive and regulatory favoritism on incentives

good, the more reluctant one should be to have the motives of government called into question regardless of who is currently in power.

Eroded faith in the rule of law directly increases uncertainty associated with cooperative activity. This raises expected transaction costs that reduce the scale and scope of viable transactions. An erosion of faith in the rule of law also reduces trust in the system by reducing faith that one will keep one's just deserts. If it is all just a big political game, why risk putting out effort or making investments? The better play is to invest in political favoritism.

When politics enters into regulatory and judicial decision-making, it undermines the rule of law. In the United States the rule of law is a matter of process, not outcomes. The US Constitution and its states' constitutions provide a means by which outcomes are considered—the legislative process. When outcomes are decided by regulatory and judicial decision-making, the door is opened for special interest group pressure to change them. This produces winners and losers, so inevitably trust in the system is eroded. Trust in the system and the rule of law are therefore inseparable—one without the other is largely meaningless.

The Dilemma

Most humans desire prosperity and freedom. But freedom requires democracy, and democracy, if only guided by rational self-interest, tends to undermine the high-trust society and therefore many of the institutions upon which free market economies and democratic governments depend. That democracy can be both a necessary condition for mass flourishing and possibly a sufficient condition for its ultimate failure constitutes quite a dilemma.

This dilemma can be ameliorated by constraining the democratic process so the Olson story can't get off the ground. Such constraints are evident in constitutions, laws, institutions, and policies. But in a genuine democracy such constraints can be modified or removed. If a society has a genuine democracy and it hopes to avoid undermining trust in the system, it must do so in some other way than mechanisms that can be altered by the democratic process.

Culture is uniquely suited for solving this problem. Like nothing else, culture can address the crux of the problem, which is the rationality of using the democratic process to promote special interests. Consider a society with prevailing moral beliefs that view opportunism as completely unacceptable and with a prevailing understanding of how democracy is intended to work to best promote the common good. In such a society people will view using the democratic process to engage in redistributive or regulatory favoritism as an immoral violation of the social contract, no matter how noble the intentions.

Conveying such moral beliefs in a cultural way so they exert their influence as tastes preempts the inexorable logic behind special interest groups promoting their welfare at the expense of the common good by constraining democratic voting at a prerational stage of decision-making. This forecloses the means by which politicians enrich themselves through vote buying that ultimately destroys trust in the system and undermines the common good.

Notes

1. There is increasing appreciation in the literature for the need to consider the role culture plays in the field of political economy. For a review, see Alesina (2013).

2. This counterintuitive argument is worked out in detail in Hilton Root's (2006) *Capital and Collusion* and Hilton Root's (2008) *Alliance Curse*.

3. See, for example, Milton Friedman's (1981) *Capitalism and Freedom* or Richard Pipes's (1999) *Property and Freedom*.

4. An exception is the Regulatory Policy Institute study *Trust in the System* (2009). Another exception is Fournier and Quinton, "How Americans Lost Trust in Our Greatest Institutions (2012). This article cites interesting Gallup poll data on the fall of trust in various institutions from 2002 to 2011.

5. See, for example, Niall Ferguson's (2008) *The Ascent of Money*.

6. This quote comes from Milton Friedman's response to a question from Robert McKenzie in the ninth volume of the PBS special series *Free to Choose*, 1980.

7. Honestly run firms also benefit from vigorous external auditing. But trust in the system arising from external audits has been eroding steadily over time as accountancy has become based more on rules than on principles out of growing fear of litigation. Laws like Sarbanes-Oxley exacerbate this trend because they give lawyers standards to follow that further reduce the risk of litigation. But it is principles-based accounting that affords discretion to hunt down and unravel, in a determined way, newly devised schemes that circumvent existing rules and laws. I thank Stephen Moehrle for clarifying the effect of Sarbanes-Oxley.

8. See Art Swift (2016) writing for Gallup.

9. Lee Kuan Yew was cofounder and first secretary-general of the People's Action Party and Singapore's first prime minister, serving from 1959 to 1960.

10. Jack Weatherford, in his book *Indian Givers: How the Indians of the Americas Transformed the World* (1988), argued that democracy was not only practiced by

Native Americans before the arrival of Europeans, it informed the Founding Fathers thinking on the design of the US constitutional government. Lars Brownworth, in his book *Sea Wolves: A History of the Vikings* (2014), similarly points out that the Vikings were very democratic.

11. See Christopher Boehm's (2012) *Moral Origins: The Evolution of Virtue, Altruism, and Shame*.

12. There are too many warnings about the limitations of democracy to reproduce here. Some of democracy's greatest advocates were well aware of its limitations. Those offering warnings include John Adams, Aristotle, Isaac Asimov, Cicero, G. K. Chesterton, Winston S. Churchill, F. A. Hayek, Robert A. Heinlein, Aldous Huxley, D. H. Lawrence, C. S. Lewis, Norman Mailer, H. L. Mencken, Plato, Elmer T. Peterson, George Bernard Shaw, Marvin Simkin, Adam Smith, Thucydides, and Oscar Wilde.

13. See also Mancur Olson's (1982) *The Rise and Decline of Nations*.

14. The difference between socially efficient redistribution and redistributive favoritism is addressed fully in chapter 8.

15. This idea was put forth most powerfully by George Stigler in "The Theory of Economic Regulation" (1971).

7

The Fall of Flourishing Societies

John Adams was famous for the tender yet deeply intellectual correspondence he had with his wife Abigail. Abigail was brilliant and Adams knew he owed much of his success to her. So it is especially troubling that in a letter to her he felt the need to express his concerns about the inherent instability of democracy. In his own words:

> Remember, democracy never lasts long. It soon wastes, exhausts, and murders itself. There never was a democracy yet that did not commit suicide. It is in vain to say that democracy is less vain, less proud, less selfish, less ambitious, or less avaricious than aristocracy or monarchy. It is not true, in fact, and nowhere appears in history. (Adams 2003)

So what role might waning culture play in opening the door to societal failure, perhaps beginning with the collapse of democratic government? This is an important question for societies, like many in the West, that are presently well described as flourishing democracies. In this chapter I hope to shed light on why it is that the more successful a country becomes, the more attention it must pay to investing in trust-producing culture so democracy does not "murder itself."

The Worsening Investment Problem

Parents have some idea of how much time children spend, on average, playing video games versus learning lessons about morality. This average establishes a norm, and from one generation to the next this norm moves slowly. The problem is that there are large benefits to be derived from avoiding some of the cost of inculcating trust-producing moral beliefs. The less time and money parents spend on such investment, the more they have for themselves and for helping their children be successful in other ways. This includes providing better nutrition, healthcare, and education. It also includes cultivating other laudable traits like charitableness, leadership, and teamwork.

At the same time, spending a little less time and money on their own children than their parents did on them will not seem to produce much of a difference in outcomes, mostly because such differences cannot be observed until it is too late. No one expects young children to be completely trustworthy no matter how well they are being raised. But by the time it is clear that a given parent did not invest enough into inculcating trust-producing moral beliefs, the child is an adult.

The costs and benefits involved are further muddied by broader social changes. I have no idea how much time and money my parents would have put into monitoring my video game, cell phone, and internet usage. It is very hard for parents to connect cause and effect between moral training, a child's chances for success, and the quality of society for the next generation because there are many complicating factors, some of which have no point of reference in any parent's own childhood.

Many factors can therefore contribute to falling investment into trust-producing moral beliefs. This does not require that parents consciously choose to do less than they know they should to best promote the common good in how they raise their own children. In most cases parents simply conform to a cultural norm for an activity that is changing so slowly that they might not even be aware that it is changing. Such change might be noticeable from generation to generation, but that is likely noticing too late.

In many societies older adults complain about the erosion of culture over the course of their lives. But by the time cultural decline is obvious to them, their grandchildren are already being raised by their own children. Of course their own children were also raised by parents who were subject to cultural decline that their children's grandparents complained about. But while they were raising their own children this, to them, looked more like innocuous cultural change or "progress" than nefarious cultural decline.

We mostly perceive of cultural decline through the rearview mirror, by what comes after us that we can observe, not by what came before us that we did not observe. But by the time the observable outcomes for the adults of generation t can be compared to the observable adult outcomes for generation $t - 1$, it is too late to change how the adults of generation t will be educated in their childhood. They will already be well on their way toward educating their own children in period t according to the new normal, which for them is simply normal. So we have the cliché of grandparents carping to their children about how they are raising their grandchildren. They issue warnings, but to the current generation of parents, such warnings fall largely on deaf ears as these parents wonder who their own parents thought raised them.

Because less investment in trust-producing moral beliefs frees up resources for other important things, the incentive to reduce investment is like gravity. In the absence of observed harm, it is inevitable that the level of investment will slowly fall over time, generation after generation, once a society is so large that reduced investment produces no perceptible effect on child success or on the high-trust society.

Since there are high immediate payoffs from reducing such investment, as long as nothing bad happens reducing such investment is copied and becomes a trend. At the same time, the larger a society becomes, the weaker is the connection between cause and effect and therefore the harder it is to see the harm that results. We are all tempted to invest a little less for the future if it frees up resources for the present, so when future benefits become hard to discern or are largely moot, less investment occurs.

So once a society becomes a truly a high-trust society, generation after generation will begin to enjoy less of the benefit of having highly trust-dependent institutions like contracts, property rights enforcement, sound money, honest voting, and the rule of law. As these institutions begin to falter, other institutions that depend on them (e.g., contractually coordinated commerce that depends on trust in the judiciary) start to falter. This erosion of the institutions we take for granted happens so slowly it goes largely unnoticed. And it can happen even in societies *in which every adult abides by trust-producing moral beliefs*.

The Worsening Political Polarization Problem

Societal Success, Growth, and the Olson Problem

Because mass flourishing requires large-group cooperation, the fall of any flourishing society begins with a large society. The larger a society is, the greater will be the number of people over which the cost of policies that favor any special interest group can be spread. This allows it to enjoy the fruits of political favoritism without causing enough harm to arouse resistance.

In very small societies this problem does not exist because there are too few others over which to spread costs, so political favoritism creates enemies as fast as it creates friends. So in the very small-group societies within which democratic practices first emerged, voting was mostly about collective choice (should we move the camp or stay put), providing public goods (do we build a fence or take our chances with raiders), rectifying other kinds of market failure problems (how far outside the camp will we require everyone to go to dump their trash), or choosing a leader to deal with problems that are either too trivial or too urgent to be dealt with through direct voting.

But the larger a society is, the more likely that special interest groups will figure out that they can benefit by using democracy to redistribute benefits to themselves because doing so will not arouse opposition. This increases the degree to which government is focused on redistributive and regulatory favoritism relative to addressing market failure problems.

As special interest groups grow in size and number, one naturally suspects that the net gains to special interest group politics will fall since the key to success is being a small group relative to society. But recall from the previous chapter that as more people join special interest groups, those not yet in such a group find it increasingly imperative to join one just to break even, because they are already paying for the favoritism others enjoy.

So as societies grow, special interest groups proliferate. They become more numerous as people feel increasingly compelled to join one or more. They become larger as a competition emerges over political influence since large special interest groups can deliver more campaign contributions and votes than small ones. This further increases their influence on the democratic process. Since this activity only reallocates resources created in the private sector, increasingly groups form just to ensure that their members get at least their fair share of the pie. This contributes to the misguided belief that free market democracies are little more than giant zero-sum games.

Government redistribution and regulation increased dramatically in the West over the 20th century. Yet in the years since Olson wrote *The Logic of Collective Action*, the majority has shown little concern for the harm that special interest group politics can do to democracy, while concern for the problem of tyranny by the majority remains very high. It seems that nothing can make the majority of voters in Western societies respond as automatically as being given a chance to express agreement that minority groups of almost any kind continue to be victims of tyranny of the majority.[1]

One explanation for this paradoxical view is that humans naturally empathize with minority groups because they have less political power than the majority. At the same time, many fail to recognize that the since those in the majority are human and therefore naturally empathic, there is little likelihood that they will use the democratic process to engage in oppression. This empathy effect is important because the larger is the majority relative to any minority group, the more likely it is that if members of the majority benefit by extracting resources from the minority group, members of the minority group will be harmed substantially.

Suppose, for example, that 95% of the population decides to extract from the remaining 5% enough money to redistribute $200 per year to each member of the majority group. This means that each member of the minority group will be harmed by the amount of $3,800 per year. If gaining $200 per person is enough to be worth the majority's effort to extract it, then surely the loss of $3,800 per person by those in the minority group constitutes a heavy burden.

Sharply self-interested models of rational political behavior ignore the effect that empathy might have. Such models suggest that those in the majority will use the power that the democratic system affords them to extract benefits from minority groups despite the great harm doing so would cause. But that is not what has happened in the West. Sharply self-interested models of rational political behavior miss the mark because they ignore the possibility that our innate sense of empathy would make the majority feel very guilty about inflicting so much harm on members of the minority group.

One could argue that racial discrimination by the majority against the minority in the United States contradicts this point. But think about what turned the tide in the civil rights movement. When mass media started putting the reality of prejudice and racism in plain view to the white majority, their sense of empathy was aroused to such a high level that it led to political pressure, from the white American majority, to address these matters in the form of the Civil Rights Act of 1957, the Civil Rights Act of 1964, the Voting Rights Act of 1965, and numerous subsequent changes in agency law.

Unfortunately, the preceding arithmetic works in precisely the opposite direction for special interest group politics. Policies that favor special interest groups often do too little harm to arouse opposition, but the benefits to members of the special interest group are concentrated enough to significantly improve their welfare while doing little harm to those in the majority. If, for example, 1% of the population is able to use the democratic process to redistribute enough resources from the remaining 99% to give themselves $200 per year per member, the cost to each member of the remaining 99% would only be $2.02 per year.

Why the Theory of Market Failure Matters

Good governance requires extracting resources from the private sector as efficiently as possible to provide resources for addressing market failure problems. By definition, the gain to society from doing so will outweigh the cost, so addressing market failure problems advances the common good. The economic theory of market failure is important precisely because it provides us with a means of discriminating between laudable causes that should be addressed by society, but not government, and problems that can only be adequately addressed by government.

Unfortunately, political incentives for addressing genuine market failure problems become weaker as a society grows. This is because addressing most market failure problems produces large but diffuse benefits across the whole of society and therefore generates no concentrated political support from special interest groups. Consider, for example, something that is of universal value, such as clean drinking water. Because clean water is of universal value, providing it benefits voters for your opponent as much as your own.

On the other hand, many special interest groups are far smaller than 1% of the voting public, so they can fit nicely on one side of the political aisle. So those in power can extract resources from the private sector to reward special interest groups for their political support through redistributive and regulatory favoritism. And as we have already seen, the larger a society is, the less likely it is that any particular instance of this activity will be noticed, let alone opposed, by the majority.

Solving a market failure problem amounts to using a dollar that could have produced a dollar's worth of social benefit in the private sector to promote far more than a dollar's worth of social benefit by being employed in, or directed by, the public sector. That such socially beneficial, utterly *positive-sum* activity does not happen on its own through voluntary transactions is precisely what it means to say that the market failed. Political favoritism, however, is not about addressing market failure and is at best a zero-sum game, and when one takes account of its effects on incentives, it is clear that political favoritism is nearly always a negative-sum game.[2]

Politicians cannot take the support they get from special interest groups for granted because other politicians compete for their support by offering more favoritism. This results in a political arms race that requires ever increasing extraction of resources from the private sector. This induces wealth creators to take ever more defensive measures, which directs ever more resources to activities like tax avoidance.

This reduces resources available for investment in productivity-increasing capital or even investment to keep up the existing capital stock. Because of this, government finds that it has to increasingly rely on unexpected changes in policy, such as constantly increasing tax rates or inventing new taxes. Such actions further increase transaction costs thereby further reducing output per capita. Such actions also reduce the trust that those who create wealth have in the system. This further reduces output per person.

So in a variety of ways, redistributive and regulatory favoritism erodes trust in the system, and increasing political competition for votes due to politicians outbidding each other year after year makes this problem worse. The effect all of this has on trust in the system is indicated by the new dashed line in figure 7.1.

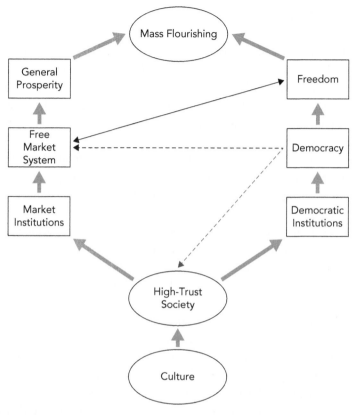

FIGURE 7.1

Adverse effect of redistributive and regulatory favoritism on trust in the system

The general lesson is that a society can start with a high level of generalized bilateral trust and trust in the system only to find that as it grows, the democratic process becomes increasingly prone to redistributive and regulatory favoritism. Such favoritism ultimately undermines trust in the system and, hence, undermines the high-trust society.

Political Tribalism

Voters are most likely to have trust in the democratic system, and therefore trust in the system in general, when the democratic process is limited to addressing market failure problems. This is because when people differ about how best to address a market failure problem, the harm done to the losing side is normally only counterfactual in nature.

Consider a street in need of repair. One group might favor topping the street with an inch of new asphalt. Another group might favor starting over with new concrete, which will last longer but is far more expensive. Although each might strongly oppose the other's approach, it is entirely possible that no matter which side wins, everyone will be better off. When addressing a genuine market failure problem, in many cases those on the losing side lose only counterfactually because their welfare will be improved by solving the problem either way.

This is very different from special interest group opportunism. If there is no market failure problem being addressed, the losing group is necessarily made worse off because resources going to the winning group come from the losers. This makes the losing side not just the losers of the vote but also losers of resources they once had. Most people can accept being on the losing side of a vote if that means someone else's idea about how to solve a market failure was chosen over theirs. But few people can accept being forced to pay for political favoritism.

As courting special interest groups becomes an increasingly important part of winning elections, politicians spend less time courting voters with policy proposals aimed at addressing market failure problems (e.g., updating water purification systems) and spend more time pledging a willingness to fight for favored groups. Politics becomes less about what a candidate is for and more about who a candidate is for. Politics becomes less about competing views of good policy and more about gaining control of resource flows to be able to mete out rewards to put together a winning coalition.

Note that this is not a problem of corruption that can be addressed by improving law enforcement. Special interest groups that use the democratic process to promote their welfare at the expense of the common good can operate fully within the letter of the law. In most cases members of such groups are completely convinced of the morality of their actions. Many view using the democratic process in this way as merely playing the political game skillfully and view those who object as inept sore losers.

The Political Sweet Spot

To engender favorable treatment, a special interest group must be large enough to produce enough campaign contributions and votes to make a difference in a candidate's chances of being elected. But it must also be small enough so that preferential policies produce noticeable gains to members while imposing costs that are too low to be noticed or, if noticed, too low to be worth opposing by the majority. So special interest groups face a trade-off. Balancing the costs and benefits of this trade-off defines a kind of political sweet spot for the size of any special interest group.

Politicians can increase the size of this sweet spot to engender more support, however, if they can provide more support without additional resources. One way to do this is to promise regulatory favoritism that does not require additional government spending. This can increase campaign contributions and votes without requiring money. But the cost of such favoritism can be very high to society. Consider, for example, an unfunded mandate that increases production costs, which are passed on to consumers through higher prices. This is essentially a hidden tax that is often blamed on firms by the very politicians who are responsible for it.

Unfortunately, there is a far more nefarious path by which politicians can increase the size of the political sweet spot for special interest groups. A politician can garner additional support by arguing that if his opponent wins, the special interest group's members will be harmed. Perhaps existing policies that favor them will be dismantled. Perhaps policies that favor the other side at their expense will be adopted.

Demonizing the other side works well because the potential harm that can be done to a given special interest group by the other side is great. More to the point, there is no cost to be spread over voters by the politician who garners support in this way. This means the special interest group can grow in size and in perceived benefit per member because the flow of benefits does not require a larger tax bill that grows in proportion to the size of the special interest group or the perceived benefit per member.

Large special interest groups can deliver more campaign contributions and votes than small ones. Special interest groups that greatly benefit their members can also deliver more campaign contributions and votes than those that only modestly benefit their members. As elections are won with ever larger special interest groups but the returns to redistributive and regulatory favoritism dwindle, this kind of demonization of the other side becomes ever more important. Words like "them" and phrases like "fight for" are clear indications of growing attempts to arouse such political tribalism.

Political Conformity

Pressure to conform to the group's standards can rise with group size.[3] Think of political party membership. The group can grow in size by pulling in more subgroups, but this increases the diversity of agendas. This requires mechanisms to compel individuals and subgroups to surrender a measure of self-interest for the good of the party. This is a rational concession if a group believes the indirect benefit from being a member of the larger group outweighs the benefit of being able to deviate from the larger group's platform. This further *promotes* political tribalism in at least two ways.

First, the group itself has its own commons dilemma to deal with. Within a special interest group, the best outcome for any individual or subgroup comes from being in the group while the individual or subgroup does whatever he or the subgroup pleases. This can destroy group effectiveness, so mechanisms are put in place to punish defection from the interest group's agenda. One avoids such punishment by always behaving as expected and always joining in on punishing those who don't. This is antithetical to individualism and diversity.[4]

Second, the value of being in the group can be increased by creating a bright line between being in or out of the group. The more that those outside the group are demonized and the more harshly they are treated, the more costly it is to be banished because one doesn't stick to the group's rules or one fails to join in on punishing others who don't.

There has always been political tribalism because tribalism works. My point is that political tribalism is likely to get even worse with the rising success of societies. This is very counterintuitive, but evidence of it is all around us. If we understand why political tribalism worsens with increasing societal success, we have a better chance of keeping it from undermining high-trust societies that support mass flourishing.

When Losing Becomes Too Costly

As the beneficiaries of redistribution become used to continuing support, demonizing is likely to become more effective. This is because such beneficiaries will feel increasingly vulnerable and therefore increasingly justified in taking action to ensure they are not harmed by having existing support withdrawn.

Voters who support candidates that direct resources toward them become more dependent on the government's power to redistribute over time. This increases the return to investment in political favoritism relative to the return to investment in human capital. So rational parents become more concerned about strong social programs for them and their children and less concerned about strong schools.

This can feed on itself to produce a culture of dependency. As human capital investment falls, individuals become less able to take care of themselves and therefore more vulnerable. This makes them increasingly willing to do whatever it takes to ensure their side wins. Given the reduction in quality of life they would experience, in part because of their low level of human capital, they increasingly view not being taken care of as an immoral outcome.

Note that even if both sides prefer having no favoritism, once polarization gets going it is hard to stop. It's increasingly a matter of us versus them. Increased polarization leads to increased paranoia. Everyone fears the other side getting into power because the other side will either expropriate from them or cut off their existing support. As competing sides get swept up in increasing paranoia, they eventually begin to take measures to ensure the other side does not win because the cost of losing is just too high.[5]

Both sides know that the other side is likely thinking the same thing, so both sides begin to worry that the other side may resort to cheating. Even if they believe that cheating is wrong, all else the same, they also believe that all else is not the same. Each side can eventually convince itself that the common good is best served by not allowing the other side to have power. Each side eventually conjectures that the other side will soon cheat if it is not doing so already. Better, then, to cheat before the other side gains so much power that it will never be given up.

This facilitates the rationalization of electoral fraud. So from mutual suspicion arising from political tribalism, trust in the democratic process can be destroyed. Collapsing faith in the democratic process can eventually lead to one or both sides to consider fascism. For those on the political extremes, it is better to have a fascist ruler who supports their side than one who supports the other. The balance is ultimately tipped when those in the middle surmise that any fascist ruler would be better than whipsawing democracy.

This feedback process comports with what the historical record tells us about the beginning of the end of many democracies. Over time the likelihood rises that there will be a left-wing or a right-wing dictator, but either way there is a dictator. This is hardly a novel line of argument. Plato, in his discussion of the five regimes in Book VIII of *The Republic*, gives a very similar account of how democracy, the fourth regime, ultimately falls apart from being used as mechanism for promoting self over the common good, leading to tyranny, the fifth regime. The effects of this process are depicted in figure 7.2.

The shortest dashed arrow represents the effect that vote buying has on undermining trust in the democratic process by undermining trust in elections being honestly run. The lower dashed arrow represents that as the democratic process itself increasingly

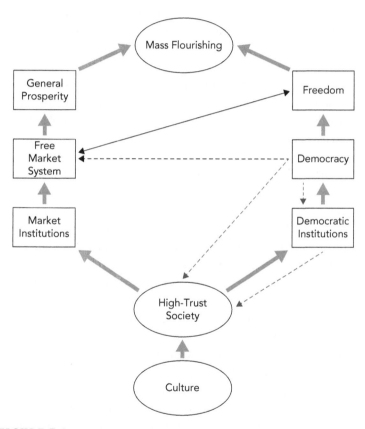

FIGURE 7.2

Adverse effect of political favoritism on trust in the democratic system, which reduces trust in the system even further

becomes a game of intrigue, the stability of the rules of the game is undermined so trust in the system is further undermined.

A Civic Role for Moral Beliefs

As explained by Christopher Boehm (2012), Bowles and Gintis (2011), and many others, in hunter-gatherer bands our highly refined communication skills made purely top down decision-making unworkable. No matter how powerful an individual might be, he was no match for three others who had worked out an agreement to put an end to his tyranny. Because of this, methods of determining consensus such as voting evolved to minimize conflict within the band.

In a small hunter-gatherer band self-serving proposals are usually transparent. Because the group is small, they will also likely harm others noticeably, so self-serving proposals are rarely offered. But in large societies things are rarely so obvious, so special interest groups naturally form to exchange campaign contributions and votes with politicians in return for support for self-serving laws and policies.

A free market democracy that is large enough to produce mass flourishing is large enough for Olson's special interest group arithmetic to lead to the democratic process being subverted for political favoritism. To be sustainable, the democratic process must be kept from this activity since it destroys trust in the system. Prevailing moral beliefs that regard this practice as inherently wrong can act as a bulwark against politicians turning the democratic process into a vote-buying machine.

Such beliefs can be complemented with the economic theory of market failure to provide a bright line of demarcation between the proper and improper use of the democratic process. Many forms of positive moral action that are not subject to market failure should be addressed by society, but "society" is not equivalent to "government." What makes government distinctive is that it has the power to compel action or inaction. Using such power outside the realm of addressing market failure necessarily involves picking winners and losers and thereby opens the door to political tribalism. Not asking for and not tolerating the use of government power in the absence of market failure can therefore be viewed of as a matter of civic duty.

Such a view was common in the United States until the middle of the 20th century and was often conveyed through the story of Davey Crockett. Davey Crockett was the only US House representative from Tennessee to oppose Andrew Jackson's Indian Removal Act of 1830. But he also spoke out against Congress making a special appropriation to benefit the widow of a national war hero (Stephen Decatur Jr.). He argued that while the impulse was laudable, it was not the proper role of government.

The Rise of Deleterious Moral Beliefs

To focus on the problem of inadequate investment in social human capital, in chapter 5 I assumed everyone in society endorsed trust-producing moral beliefs. This unrealistic assumption allowed me to show that even under the most favorable cultural content conditions, there will still be inadequate inculcation of trust-producing moral beliefs. I now consider factors that might lead parents to teach their children other moral beliefs.

Individual Effects

As a society becomes high trust in nature, one's children are increasingly likely to be presumed trustworthy. So if they are careful opportunists, they'll enjoy higher payoffs than if they strictly adhere to duty-based moral restraint. This means that parents may come to conclude that strict adherence to duty-based moral restraint might not be in their children's best interest. Moral beliefs that permit the rationalization of opportunism in the case of golden opportunities will produce superior payoffs given the skyrocketing returns to opportunism from the convention of presumptively extending trust to strangers.

In a very large, complex, and prosperous society, parents will also notice that some adults are able to prosper greatly by skirting the rules, so perhaps they are not doing their own children a service by leaving them zero ability to rationalize such actions. Even for parents who care deeply about their own children, there is the additional consideration of the role that beliefs play in helping their own children succeed relative to others.[6]

This need not necessarily be an overtly strategic decision by parents. Whereas prior generations might have strongly inculcated an ethic of duty-based moral restraint, the current generation might treat moral decision-making as too complicated to be adequately considered with a simple rule (isn't stealing bread OK if you are starving?). Remember that harm-based moral restraint comes most naturally to us, so all that is required for this belief to rise in importance is anything less than a strong emphasis on duty-based moral restraint.

Group-Level Effects

To the extent that a rapidly growing free market democracy owes its growth to a high-trust society, there will be skyrocketing returns to rational opportunism. This is because a convention of presumptively extending trust and the absence of institutions to combat opportunism combine to make fertile ground for opportunists.

Groups that possess moral beliefs that do not stress duty-based moral restraint will therefore likely experience ever higher payoffs as a society reaches ever higher levels of trust and prosperity. Such groups would therefore be expected to grow from within as well as through intermarriage, since individuals and their parents favor richer mates.

This problem can be exacerbated by the political process. Groups that hold moral beliefs that forbid using the democratic process to engage in political opportunism will have lower payoffs than groups whose moral beliefs do not. So the greater the extent to which resource allocation is mediated by political forces, the more likely the latter kinds of groups will grow relative to the former kinds of groups in both influence and size.

Corruption

Many citizens in democracies complain about corrupt politicians. So why don't they just vote them out? When the democratic process is not bridled by moral beliefs that forbid engaging in redistributive and regulatory favoritism, the stakes involved in any given election grow larger over time. Eventually so much is on the line that it becomes imperative that your candidate is re-elected.

This means that the cost of insisting that elected officials exhibit laudable traits like wisdom, leadership, integrity, and so forth rises dramatically. When your own representative or senator is caught doing something unethical, you'd better think twice before punishing him by voting for someone else since it might mean losing benefits you have secured from his role in the government.

Bryan Caplan has explained why for most individuals this will not make a difference, since most voters actually do vote their conscience. But part of the reason why they vote their conscience is that there is a very low cost from doing so because the probability of an individual's vote determining an election is miniscule.[7] This is not necessarily true for a special interest group since it can deliver blocs of votes and can also make sizeable campaign contributions. As special interest groups proliferate over time, then, an unbridled democracy is likely to look less like a collective choice mechanism than a spoils system.

Where institutional bridles such as constitutions still do a relatively good job ensuring that democracy is used as intended, it is easy to take them for granted. This is because bridles do their job by keeping things from happening, so there is no direct cause to match up with effects. The benefits of bridling democracy are most directly reflected in evidence that takes the form of the dog that didn't bark, political opportunism that did not happen, and high-trust societies that did not fade.

But there is indirect evidence. Redistributive and regulatory favoritism amounts to a zero-sum game. Zero-sum games bring out the worst in people. As people become more convinced that those in other political parties are out to benefit themselves at others' expense, things can become very ugly indeed. This ugliness is increasingly on display in free market democracies that redistribute increasing amounts of resources and control increasing amounts of behavior over time.

Virtually no one expects unbridled capitalism to work well. History shows that unbridled democracy does not work well, either. Institutional bridles such as constitutions can help save democracy from itself, but in a genuine democracy such institutions can be changed by voters. Culture provides the only durable way to address this problem because it is the only bridle that gets to the root of the problem, which is the voters themselves. Free market democracies therefore have the best chance of spoiling Plato's prediction when they are filled with citizens who believe it is their civic and moral duty not to use, and not to tolerate others using, the democratic process in the absence of market failure.

Notes

1. This is not a reference to racial minority groups. It refers to any kind of group that is smaller than the majority of voting citizens.

2. This is not to say that political activism does not attempt to address market failure problems. But the word "favoritism" is used intentionally to draw a contrast between political activism in general—some of which clearly advances the common good—and political favoritism, which for the reasons already given does not.

3. Note that gains from larger group size produce incentives for societies to suppress tribalism within them, but not across them. Very large societies have used tribalism to reduce the effects of empathy, which gets in the way of brutality.

4. This, unfortunately, comports with increasing pressure on faculty and students to obey conventions of political correctness, even so far as to result in the adoption of speech codes at many colleges and universities today.

5. Political polarization is not new, of course, but it appears to be growing. In *It's Even Worse Than it Looks* (2012), Thomas Mann and Norman Ornstein document the rapidly growing level of dysfunction from the growing political extremism in Washington, DC. This has been growing some time and almost a decade later the aftermath of the 2016 election has seen an acceleration in hyper-partisanship. Such

growing extremism and rancor has all the signs of political tribalism feeding on itself.

6. I return to this issue in chapter 9.

7. See Bryan Caplan's (2007) *The Myth of the Rational Voter* for a discussion of a broad array of evidence that indicates that most people do not engage in voting behavior that comports with strict rationality.

8

Family, Religion, Government, and Civilization

This book has explained how trust-producing culture can channel rationality in a way that creates and sustains high-trust societies that best support mass flourishing. Along the way I have kept discussion of implications to a minimum. I now address some of the implications my analysis has on the topics of family, religion, and government.

Family

When humans are children their brains are particularly receptive to learning. With very young children especially, learning is better described as absorbing information than as choosing to believe. What is learned in early childhood also frames how everything is learned thereafter, how it is interpreted, and how it is integrated into a child's evolving conceptions of right and wrong. One reason why families are so important is that early childhood presents societies with a short window of opportunity to teach to a highly receptive mind. Parents are obviously in a uniquely powerful position to make the most of this window.

Thus far I have implicitly treated children as mere objects of parental affection. Parents invest in their children because they love them and therefore want them to live good lives. But through most of human history children were also important inputs to household production. When children contributed to family welfare (e.g., six-year-olds gather eggs, seven-year-olds milk cows, nine-year-olds pick beans, and so forth), parents had a strong incentive to inculcate traits that make children good workers as early as possible.[1] Virtues like always keeping one's word were not just laudable moral ideals, they helped ensure children could be trusted with important jobs.

Because of the range of activities required to run a family farm, the additional division of labor afforded by having more children often led to productivity gains that could more than cover their cost. This was due, in part, to children being less expensive to raise in the past. There was not much reading, writing, or arithmetic to teach a nine-year-old peasant child in medieval Europe and certainly no need to save for college. So not so long ago children were a good investment for many families and the sooner they were able to work, the greater would be the return on that investment.

Parents didn't feel guilty about this practice because they believed it would ultimately benefit their children in adulthood. Families therefore rather automatically produced trustworthy workers. To the extent that family investment into trust-producing moral beliefs helps foster and sustain the high-trust society and thereby produces additional returns for society as a whole, such human capital is also effectively social capital. So the direct benefits to the family of investing early and heavily into inculcating trust-producing moral beliefs may have helped offset the problem of inadequate investment discussed in chapter 5.

This may help explain the decline in measured trust and trustworthiness in the West. As recently as the early 20th century, there were many important jobs children could do at a fairly young age, especially if they were trustworthy. The earlier they could be trusted, the sooner the family would benefit from their labor. But technological advances have affected this means of overcoming the insufficient investment problem in at least two ways.

First, improvements in technology have mechanized most of the menial tasks that we once delegated to children, so they have become less important as inputs to production. Picking machines and automated mass production pushed children out of agricultural and industrial production. A century ago a nine-year-old would trod out to the barn to milk the cows every morning. Today, however, no one would trust a nine-year-old to run a line of high-tech milking machines. There is far less that children can do to contribute to household production today, so the return to inculcating traits like trustworthiness as early in childhood as possible has fallen.

Second, the more technologically advanced a society is, the more formal education people must have to be net contributors to society. A century ago most children could start contributing significantly to the family as early as nine years of age. Many would require no additional schooling after they reached 12 years of age, so they could begin work full time in the field or in the factory to help support the family.

But now most children remain in school well into adulthood. So over the 20th century the number of years a family could benefit from their own children's labor fell dramatically. Technological advances decreased the number of things young children could do, while it increased the amount of schooling they needed to be productive. Over time the number of years that the average child was a net financial drain on the average family increased.

As the payback period to the family from inculcating traits that make good workers grew shorter, the incentive for parents to invest in such traits grew weaker. Increasingly investment in such traits was driven solely by parental love. So the insufficient investment story laid out in chapter 5 became an increasingly accurate description of reality over the course of the 20th century.

The effect that using child labor on family farms had on human capital investment might also help explain the extraordinary success of countries like the United States. Until the middle of the 19th century, the United States was still predominantly an agricultural society. But a much higher proportion of adults owned their own farms in the United States than in Europe. The typical American lived and worked on a farm owned by his or her own family. Therefore American farmers had much more to gain for their families than European farmers did from inculcating into their children the kinds of virtues that would make them better workers.

This also meant that the typical American farmer had much more to gain than the typical European farmer from innovation, investment, and hard work. So while Europe enjoyed the emergence of an entrepreneurial spirit in its relatively small merchant class, the United States enjoyed the emergence of an entrepreneurial spirit among the majority of its citizens. America was a nation filled with farm owners. As such, it was a nation filled with business owners. The children of American farmers observed their parent's behavior and thought it only natural to be optimistic about what happens when one is innovative, willing to invest, and hardworking.

So while the Protestant ethic was at the root of what Deirdre McCloskey described as *The Great Enrichment*, it was in America that an entrepreneurial spirit existed among the majority of citizens. This might help explain why America came to have such a highly creative, optimistic, and entrepreneurial culture even in comparison to the countries that invented the free market institutions that made America possible.

Religion

Most religions make the transmission of cultural knowledge more systematic than otherwise, which improves the consistency of learned moral beliefs. An organized religion can also economize on the teaching of moral beliefs by sharing fixed costs. A father who teaches his child moral beliefs every morning could almost as easily teach a group of thirty children.

Group Size and the Evolution of Religion

Most scholars now believe that the earliest religions were more focused on providing scientific beliefs about how the world works to reduce anxiety about the unknown than on providing moral beliefs about right and wrong. Religions in the earliest societies tended to emphasize the former over the latter, but as humans organized themselves into ever larger groups, the latter became increasingly important for channeling rationality to keep it from undermining the common good.[2]

This makes sense. The farther back in time one considers, the poorer our scientific understanding of the natural world was, so the more mysterious the world appeared. At the same time, we still lived in very small groups, so cooperation was already well supported by our small-group genes. The absence of beliefs about right and wrong that could help sustain large-group trust was not problematic because in early human history there were no large-group societies.

Over time competition between groups naturally led to increasing group size because gains from cooperation rise dramatically with group size. In many cases larger groups forced smaller groups to also become larger or disappear. Competition between groups therefore inevitably turned to a new margin of natural selection, which was increasing the efficiency of large-group cooperation. Concepts like duty and honor, for example, were belief mutations that made it possible for people in a large group who didn't know each other personally to be able to count on each other in very difficult circumstances, like holding a line upon attack.

Such concepts made large-group cooperation more efficient, so they spread. No one knows when this began, but the historical record suggests it began at least as far back as the early Greek city-states. Many of these familiar ideas were repeated by Rome. When we think of ancient Greece and Rome, we normally think of their magnificent buildings and enduring institutions, but the former could not have been afforded by, and the latter had no reason to evolve in, small-group societies. In short, competition between ever larger groups led to rising returns to ideas that improved the efficiency of large-group cooperation.

Many of the virtues that made large-group cooperation more efficient and can therefore be properly regarded as social capital, and not merely human capital, were exemplified by the unique personalities and capabilities of various gods. Greece had gods that were clearly more human in appearance and behavior than the gods of more primitive societies. Gods that looked like us and behaved like us but were perfect in some specific way helped increase the efficiency of large-group cooperation by providing precise models for emulation. Plato's concept of Forms, which stresses the existence of an ideal to be strived for, echoes this religious innovation.

Emulating these gods carried with it the prospect of gaining their favor. Parents therefore had an incentive to encourage their children to internalize the virtues that various gods exemplified. Among other things, Aristotle's virtue ethics reflected a shift in religion from merely currying favor with gods to changing the basic values that guide how children think and therefore how they act. The larger the social context within which behavior normally occurred, the more important were character traits that can mediate social behavior.

Over time, consistently proper behavior became increasingly understood to be less about getting right the precise response to any specific circumstance in automatic fashion and more about inculcating moral values and virtues that provide an efficacious backdrop for a reasoned approach to moral decision-making. Through the teaching and learning of moral values and virtues, religion became increasingly about cultivating good moral character, which naturally led to good behavior.

Good behavior arising from good moral character had an important advantage over good behavior arising from automatic obedience of moral rules. When an individual's morality is cultivated through moral character rather than strict obedience to "if-then" rules for behavior, a foundation exists for reasoning through what is the best moral course of action even in the face of novel circumstances. The more complex and dynamic a society is, the greater is the advantage to having moral behavior derived from reason based on moral principles and consideration of circumstances rather than a formulaic obedience of "if-then" moral rules for behavior.

Societies whose parents and civic organizations worked hardest to ensure the inculcation of such virtues enjoyed a survival advantage. This increased the size of groups in which trust could be sustained and therefore within which high-powered cooperation could occur. As religions continued to evolve, those that stumbled onto inculcating virtues that stressed duty to the larger group over oneself did even better. At the same time those that stressed moral restraint over moral advocacy did even better. Societies that put these concepts together most fully thereby produced the strongest prevailing ethic of duty-based moral restraint, resulting in their becoming the highest-trust societies.

Because of the awesome power of efficient large-group cooperation, societies that best supported large-group trust enjoy an advantage over other societies. But recall that the kind of moral beliefs that are most likely to produce large-group trust have properties that make them the least likely to enjoy adequate investment. How, then, can societies solve this problem?

Religion as Solution to the Insufficient Investment Problem

Recall that the root of the insufficient investment problem is the nonexcludability of many of the benefits of living in a high-trust society. If a society can find a way to keep people from benefiting from living in a high-trust society if their parents underinvested in trust-producing moral beliefs, such excludability would alleviate this problem. Obviously, such an approach would strike most people as unfair. But perhaps some societies stumbled upon a more palatable way to produce excludability through the evolution of religion.[3]

Recall that there is no amount of parental concern for child welfare and no level of moral earnestness that will result in a level of parental investment into trust-producing moral beliefs that best promotes the common good. This is because much of the benefit of living adulthood in a high-trust society is nonexcludable, and parents also value investing in their children in other ways. But even high payoffs from behaving as an opportunist in a high-trust society pale in comparison to the prospect of being denied happiness for eternity. This is especially true if it is contrasted with the prospect of being consigned to misery for eternity.

The existence of a belief in an afterlife can change the stakes for parents significantly if they care about the welfare of their children. Now if a parent fails to invest enough into inculcating moral beliefs in his child to satisfy the requirements of his religion, he increases the risk that his child will, as an adult, behave in ways that will lead to being denied paradise and perhaps even consigned to misery *forever*. So religion can create metaphysical excludability to replace the nonexcludability of many of the benefits of living in a high-trust society. This can potentially remove the wedge between the level of investment resulting from a consideration of the private benefits and costs involved and the level that best promotes the common good.

When there are many gods, there is no particular reason why each god who exemplifies each virtue could not be able to deny an afterlife in paradise. But without additional information, humans can only presume that all gods expect a great deal of exemplification of their respective traits. On earth, moral and virtuous behavior is often costly and resources are scarce, so choices must be made. Since even remarkably moral persons can reach different conclusion about which moral values and virtues matter most in any given circumstance, they will make different choices. This makes meaningful moral standards for behavior impossible.

Producing a trustworthy person requires more than his valuing moral restraint. It requires that moral restraint take strict precedence over moral advocacy. If traits were represented by separate gods, this required hierarchy would be left to the subjective judgment of individuals. If these traits are found in a single God, however, how that single God logically organized the relationship between moral values can also be emulated. In this way monotheism may have increased the efficiency of the cultural transmission of subtler aspects of trust-producing moral beliefs.

So religions went from being largely scientific beliefs to reduce anxiety to focusing ever more on matters of right and wrong. Some then evolved a nonmoral belief in the afterlife, which helped overcome the nonexcludability problem. Some then rolled key moral traits into a single God, which had the effect of conveying not just a set of moral values and virtues but also imbuing a logical structure on them. Some then did so in a way that made moral restraint primary to moral advocacy, thereby effectuating an ethic of duty-based moral restraint. This unleashed the gains from cooperation on an unprecedented scale.[4]

Christianity

Jesus didn't just exemplify a list of moral values and virtues. The choices he made and the rationale he gave for them also imbued a particular logical relationship between those moral values and virtues. Emulating Jesus therefore automatically results in also emulating that particular logical structure. If one is a Christian, one does not get to choose which traits to emulate or how much to emphasize one over the other.

Christianity produced another cultural innovation. The existence of *God as human* is a perplexing proposition. But since Jesus was both God and human, Christianity provided a model that could be directly imitated by humans, thereby effectively employing the powerful cultural mechanism of imitation of practices. Moreover, consistency between humans is more easily achieved by all humans imitating a single exemplar than through pairwise imitation.

Many scholars have emphasized that the Catholic Church's long-held animosity toward efforts to accumulate wealth impeded the rise of capitalism. They argued that the rise of Protestantism helped displace that impediment in Europe, and over time it also did so to some extent in countries that remained predominantly Catholic.

As efforts to accumulate wealth became increasingly regarded as morally legitimate, the government could no longer argue that wealth acquired through industriousness was morally dubious so government could justify its appropriation. In societies in which those in government were Protestants themselves, a new respect for honestly earned wealth by government likely reduced the fear of appropriation. This would have significantly increased trust in the system.

Terrorism

Those who dismiss religious terrorism as irrational do not appreciate the power of culture. Culture does not work through persuasion based on the rational application of logic and reason to evidence. Culture works by encoding ideas through tastes that are, by definition, in no way irrational because they are antecedent to rational decision-making.

There is an old saw that says you can't reason someone off of a position that wasn't reasoned to in the first place. This is precisely the problem that terrorism rooted in religious zeal presents us, because it works through tastes that people have but probably cannot remember how, when, or where they acquired them.

Some leaders of free market democracies insist on treating terrorism as an idiosyncratic threat produced by deranged minds. Others view it as a kind of mass hysteria. There is nothing we can do about idiosyncratic insanity, but we might be able to address a problem rooted in mass hysteria by appealing to rationality. But one cannot fix a problem by appealing to rationality if there is nothing irrational about the behavior that is producing the problem.

This appears to be a rather dismal observation, but by working out the precise nature of the problem, one can see a reason for hope. The idea that moral restraint should take strict precedence over moral advocacy is not inconsistent with any of the world's major religions. It is even weakly alluded to by them.[5] If we can advance a message of the wisdom of duty-based moral restraint, it might act as a meme that induces subsequent changes to religious narratives that make it harder to suppress empathy. This would make it harder to convince individuals to engage in acts of terror.

Government

I have painted a dim picture of how the democratic process can be transformed from serving as a collective choice mechanism for addressing market failure problems to being used to promote the welfare of special interest groups at the expense of the common good. Once that line is crossed, a society risks having the democratic process being used to engage in redistributive and regulatory favoritism. This pits groups against each other and therefore risks fanning the flames of political tribalism.

When a society uses the democratic process to engage in redistributive or regulatory favoritism, it descends into a zero-sum game that forces even those who disapprove of the practice to join in or serve as the greater fool. Even when such favoritism is a well-intentioned attempt to help those less fortunate, it erodes trust in the system. This reduces general prosperity for future generations and thereby reduces their ability to take care of needy persons. This amounts to choosing to promote the welfare of today's poor at the expense of tomorrow's poor.

Protecting versus Promoting Welfare

To avoid destroying trust in the system, free market democracies should inculcate the belief that it is immoral to use the democratic process to engage in redistributive or regulatory favoritism no matter how noble the ultimate objective. This ensures that democracy is only used as it was intended to be used.[6]

There is no substitute for having such a belief. In a genuine democracy any institutional constraint can be changed by voters through the democratic process. The ultimate solution therefore lies with the voters themselves. They must refuse to use the system in this way, and they must keep others from doing so. It is hard to say no to noble endeavors, so this position must be held with great conviction. Such a conviction can be derived from a deep appreciation for why such a position is required to protect democracy from itself.

A simple way to articulate this position is to envision an impenetrable wall between the protection of welfare and the promotion of welfare. In short, government power can only be used to protect welfare, never to promote it. When government attempts to promote the welfare of any individual or group, it effectively picks winners and losers, pitting the latter against the former.

But is it not a proper function of the US government to promote welfare? The preamble of the US Constitution, after all, includes the phrase "promote the general Welfare." I submit that the *only* way to promote the general welfare is *never* to promote the welfare of any individual or group. Government produces mass flourishing not by moving resources around but by catalyzing the wealth-creating activities of its citizens by addressing market failure problems. Such activity does not exist to promote the welfare of any individual or group. It exists to create an environment that best promotes the common good.

When government only protects welfare, this is of direct benefit to everyone because everyone prefers not being harmed by other individuals, groups, or government. And everyone benefits from living in a high-trust rather than a low-trust society. But while this approach produces a more limited government, it does not necessarily result in smaller government. It is entirely possible for a society that refuses to use government power to promote the welfare of any individual or group to have a very high level of government spending and regulation.

Good Government

Levying taxes to address market failure problems is not harmful to a market economy or high-trust society. When we use the democratic process to solve genuine market failure problems, we leave a richer society for the next generation, one that can afford to do even more for those in need. We do not choose the welfare of today's poor over tomorrow's poor.

In most cases people attending to their own welfare best promotes the common good, so in most cases it is unwise to manipulate private behavior. When economists say the market fails, they are referring to situations in which theory tells us that voluntary private behavior will not automatically lead to an outcome that best promotes the common good. In cases of market failure, then, the use of government power to supersede economic forces can, when properly applied, dramatically improve the common good.

When markets fail to best promote social welfare and government power is used to alter the pattern of resource allocation to improve efficiency, this often results in redistribution of income or wealth *as a byproduct*. But there is an important difference between redistribution in an effort to favor one group over another in a vote-buying exercise and redistribution that is a byproduct of addressing a genuine market failure problem. The former tends to destroy trust in democracy and ultimately trust in the system, while the latter does quite the opposite.

When, for example, an individual benefits from a Social Security survivor benefit payment, income is redistributed from society to the individual. But the purpose of this program is not to engage in redistributive favoritism to benefit a special interest group, it is to provide insurance that can potentially benefit everyone. When the federal government buys fighter aircraft, money flows from Washington to just a few states. But the purpose of the program is not to engage in redistribution to benefit a special interest group, it is to provide national defense that benefits everyone.

In both cases there are winners and losers, but the ultimate purpose of these programs is not to fund winners at the expense of losers to buy campaign contributions and votes, but to address a genuine market failure problem. Addressing these problems is not an exercise in favoritism even if it inevitably promotes the welfare of some groups more than others, or improves the welfare of some groups while reducing the welfare of others.

Moral beliefs that forbid using the democratic process to engage in redistributive or regulatory favoritism don't conflict with having a variety of social safety nets necessitated by market failure. Friedrich Hayek, Milton Friedman, and Ronald Reagan, all champions of the free market system, supported social safety nets. They understood that endorsing the use of government power to address problems of market failure is very different from endorsing the use of government to provide a means by which individuals or groups can promote their own welfare or noble agendas at the expense of the common good.

This brings us back to the principle that the only way to promote the common good through democratic government is to refuse to promote the welfare of any individual or group. Government should instead endeavor to protect the welfare of all individuals and groups. When social insurance is limited to ensuring that everyone has their basic needs met, this protects everyone from misery. That does not pit us against each other.

Civilization

Duty-based moral restraint addresses two deep problems—the empathy problem and the greater-good rationalization problem—and thereby makes it rational for individuals to be trustworthy. This produces the ultimate substrate of a high-trust society and therefore mass flourishing. But that is not all that duty-based moral restraint does. The ethic of duty-based moral restraint is the key to the civilization of our species.

Moral behavior is about doing that which is good and not doing that which is bad. Some believe that good people are people with only good impulses and few if any bad impulses. But there are bad impulses we all share by virtue of being a small-group species. Our small-group genes help us see how to promote our welfare at the expense of other persons and the common good, and our genes urge us to strongly consider doing so when the expected cost is sufficiently low. In the large-group societies upon which all civilizations are built, circumstances in which we can put self ahead of the group or society present themselves rather frequently.

Evolution ensures that all normally functioning people have both good impulses and bad impulses. Creating civilization is not about making people willing to act on their good impulses. In the large contexts required for civilization, we don't have sufficient resources to increase the welfare of the thousands of other people with whom we need to be able to directly or indirectly cooperate. Civilization, instead, depends on making people unwilling to act on their bad impulses. The closer a society can get to having people not act on bad impulses—that is, to having a very strong ethic of duty-based moral restraint—the more civilized the society will be, the higher will be its level of social trust, and the more it will support mass flourishing.

Duty-based moral restraint is derived from a created neural architecture built up through learning, because there has been very little time for genetic traits to evolve to support it. So if we are to have a prevailing ethic of duty-based moral restraint, it will have to come from the transmission of moral beliefs, generation after generation, that effectuate such a way of thinking. The *cultural* transmission of such beliefs early in childhood has the effect of making them exquisitely reliable by encoding the required behavior as tastes.

Societies differ in the degree to which their respective cultures cultivate this ethic. Societies also differ in the degree to which they are civilized. We tend to equate civilization with physical evidence of having moved to a higher level of material existence—that is, buildings and monuments—and with durable institutions that have been written down such as laws. But this is a mere shadow of what "civilized" really means. A truly civilized society is not defined by buildings, monuments, or formal institutions, it is defined by how people treat each other. In a truly civilized society, nearly everyone *behaves in a civilized manner*, meaning that all can move about with little fear except those whose actions threaten this condition.

No individual in a large society has the ability to noticeably improve the welfare of everyone else in society because positive moral action requires resources and resources are limited. Luckily that is not required for civilization. If it were, there would be no civilizations. But every individual in a large society has the ability to refrain from behavior that directly harms others because this requires inaction and therefore no additional resources. Every individual in a large society also has the ability to refrain from behavior that indirectly harms others by undermining the common good, such as by behaving in an untrustworthy way that harms no individual but nevertheless erodes the cultural commons of the high-trust society as insidiously as an extra mouthful of grass erodes Hardin's common pasture.

The key to it all is that moral restraint can be followed as a matter of duty. There are exceptions, times when morality compels costly action, but an endless obsession with exceptions blinds us from understanding that which matters most in the other 99.9% of the cases. Those who possess an ethic of duty-based moral restraint and understand why such a prevailing ethic is so important for civilized society have little trouble recognizing genuine exceptions. No one thinks that those who hid Anne Frank's family faced a genuine ethical challenge in deciding whether they should lie to the Nazis. The challenge was in whether they would have the courage to do so.

Notes

1. Children as young as 12 were often employed as apprentices in a family business. See Gary Walton and Hugh Rockoff's (2014, 59), *History of the American Economy*.

2. For an extensive review of this argument, see Lizzie Wade's "The Birth of Moralizing Gods" (2015).

3. Whether this was by design through a God or gods, was by design by some religious leaders, or was simply a random mutation that proved prepotent is irrelevant to the argument that follows.

4. For a more general argument that comports with this claim, see David Sloan Wilson's (2002) *Darwin's Cathedral*, which contends that religion likely evolved to facilitate greater cooperation.

5. The clearest example is the teaching of Hillel (ללה), a towering figure in Judaism. He famously proclaimed:

> That which is hateful to you, do not do to your fellow [man]. That is the whole Torah; the rest is the explanation; go and learn.

This statement is not identical to, but is clearly consistent with, duty-based moral restraint.

6. In his book *From Liberty to Democracy* (2002), Randall Holcombe argued that the US government went from emphasizing protection of freedom through constitutional constraints to emphasizing the democratic process itself. This accelerated with the Progressives, who viewed a government that was focused on protection of welfare as insufficient.

9

Conclusion

According to Jon Elster, "Institutions keep society from falling apart, provided there is something to keep institutions from falling apart" (Elster 1989, 147). These are wise words indeed. In my view that "something" is culture. For the institutions of a thriving free market democracy it is, more precisely, culture that instantiates a prevailing ethic of duty-based moral restraint.

Individuals, acting on self-interest alone, will not rationally choose moral beliefs for themselves that produce an ethic of duty-based moral restraint, since that would foreclose acting on future golden opportunities. But what if all the adults of each generation teach their children such an ethic? If they are taught early, often, and with great conviction, something important happens. In all but the rarest of circumstances, the adults of the next generation won't even consider behaving in an untrustworthy way. Accordingly, they will form the substrate of a high-trust society.

It is often the case with evolution what seems to be a disadvantage can work out to be an advantage in a surprising way. The need to reteach moral beliefs each and every generation makes culture fragile, but it also separates the decision to have certain kinds of beliefs from the cost of having them. This allows a society to encode certain kinds of beliefs as moral tastes that function prerationally, so individual rationality does not undermine the common good. This is what makes culture so powerful and why there is no substitute for what it does.

Free market democracies are humankind's best invention. That is a very bold statement given the obvious power of inventions like antibiotics, the internet, microchips, nuclear power, steam engines, and so forth. But think for a moment about where most of these kinds of inventions come from. They come from free market democracies. And they came at breakneck speed compared to the rate of invention before the rise of free market democracies. They came faster in free market democracies than in all other kinds of societies over the last two centuries. Free market democracies spur invention and make the benefits of inventions available to mass markets to engender even more invention, innovation, and therefore economic growth. Even other kinds of countries benefit from massive spillover effects.

The richer a society is, the easier everything becomes, including things we normally don't think of when we think of free market economic activity. The power of flexible, large-group cooperation coupled with the political stability afforded by a healthy democracy opens the door to nearly everything else. Basic scientific research, the arts, environmental protection, public education, universal healthcare, and so on, are all things that less developed countries pay far less attention to because they cannot afford to do so. A good society needs resources, and these resources are simply more available in thriving free market democracies.

Free market democracies produce mass flourishing in sustainable fashion because they don't need to produce prosperity through enslavement of their own citizens or those in other societies. Free market democracy can work for everyone in every society and for all societies at the same time because they are abuzz with cooperation that promotes the common good. And this they do ever better over time because as wellsprings of artistic creativity, scientific investigation, and entrepreneurial innovation, they are juggernauts of economic growth and development.

Many of the institutions required for a free market democracy require a high-trust society. Those who have lived their entire lives in a high-trust society naturally take trust and trust-dependent institutions for granted. Trust is to them what water is to fish, and everyone knows that fish are the last to discover water. But while the fish and water analogy conveys how easy it is underappreciate trust, the analogy is far from perfect.

Fish don't create water and they don't need to attend to it to preserve it. The high-trust society, however, a product of a cultural commons that must be carefully attended to generation after generation. So while fish can get away with taking water for granted, we who live in high-trust societies cannot get away with taking culture for granted. Unfortunately, attending to culture is hard work and requires genuine sacrifice because the investment of any given generation benefits not itself but the next.

It would seem plausible that parental concern for their children's welfare could overcome the cost of bearing this sacrifice. But, incredibly, no amount of parental concern is enough to produce a high-trust society. This is because many of the benefits of living in a high-trust society will be enjoyed by their children no matter what parents do. At the same time, there are other things they can do with their resources that increase the likelihood of success of their children.

Thriving free market democracies are therefore not natural outcomes of social, political, and economic development. Even under ideal circumstances, the deck is stacked against them. Thriving free market democracies are the products of massive intergenerational investment into the inculcation of trust-producing moral beliefs. Most societies have not been able to achieve this feat. Those that have find that as they continue to grow and prosper, they must deal with a deck that becomes increasingly stacked against their keeping it up.

It is therefore a mistake to infer from cross-sectional differences of success among societies that they are simply at different points along the same development continuum. Different societies have different prevailing moral beliefs. Different societies also have different levels of investment into the inculcation of moral beliefs. Some kinds of moral beliefs are inimical to sustaining high-trust societies, and in societies in which such beliefs prevail, greater investment into inculcating them decreases the likelihood of success.

Those who think we are naturally inclined to get along well in large-group contexts like New York City make the same mistake that fish do about water. They enjoy the benefits of thousands of years of refined trust-producing moral beliefs, thousands of hours of their parents', pastors', and teachers' time, and thousands of dollars of their parents' and society's money. And because they are oblivious, they feel no obligation to give to the next generation what was given to them.

The search for theories of trust rooted in our genes has been an understandable effort to explain trust in the most general way possible. We have indeed gotten much better at explaining small-group trust, but that is quite beside the point. It is large-group trust that is rare and powerful and therefore urgently in need of understanding. The fact that the study of small-group trust is more amenable to rigorous scientific inquiry is irrelevant.

Just as fish utterly depend on water, we who live in flourishing societies utterly depend on trust. We should therefore invest in the kind of moral beliefs that make trustworthiness possible by stressing duty-based moral restraint above all else. Moral advocacy is very important, but it can never become a rationalization for opportunism no matter how noble the intentions involved. Effectuating redistributive and regulatory favoritism through the veneer of the democratic process does not morally legitimize it. History is filled with examples of horrible decisions and policies made possible by democracy.

What Is Happening to the West?

The rise of the West is one of the great stories of human history. We continue to live well in the West and there is still much to be optimistic about in the West. But it is impossible to deny that the West is now under stress. Many view this as good news because they believe its success was largely the result of a long history of the strong oppressing the weak.

This is deeply mistaken. There will always be those who promote their welfare at the expense of the weak. Evolutionary theory assures us that such individuals and groups are inevitable. In free market democracies there will be individuals and groups who prosper by taking advantage of others in that context. In centrally planned societies there will be individuals and groups who will prosper by taking advantage of others in that context.

It is easy to see scoundrels in free market democracies because there is so much low-hanging fruit to grab. And because free market democracies are open societies, such behavior is widely reported by a free press. So inferring that widespread opportunism is a product of free enterprise is all wrong. The story starts with scoundrels because evolution guarantees we'll always have them. The story ends with the context they find themselves in.

I submit that most of the stress on the West began with the waning of what was once relatively strong culture. This has produced an erosion of trust that is now undermining the institutions of free market democracy, not the other way around. The real problem is that we have been paying inadequate attention to keeping up the cultural commons, and it shows.

Societies in the West are now transmitting far less of the kind of social human capital that sustains high-trust societies than they used to. As a result, trust and trustworthiness have declined, and so a pervasive uncertainty and suspicion hangs in the air that is suppressing optimism and is stoking cynicism. This drives trust to smaller groups and becomes an excuse for political opportunism that makes winners out of losers. In so doing, it begets tribalism. Evidence of this is everywhere, and it appears to be growing rapidly worse.

The reduction in social human capital investment is easy to underestimate because, in many families, investment in total human capital has actually increased. But we are increasingly failing to distinguish between human capital that increases the productivity of individuals and *social* human capital that produces the high-trust society. To borrow from David Brooks's *The Road to Character* (2015), we are increasingly focused on the "resume virtues" at the expense of the "eulogy virtues." Because we don't pay enough attention to this difference, the substitution of the former for the latter goes largely unnoticed.

Concern for status exacerbates this problem. In *Luxury Fever* (1999), Robert Frank pointed out that concern for status has the effect of reducing the amount of resources put toward public goods. Similarly, parental concern for the success of their own children relative to the children of others might reduce the level of investment into trust-producing moral beliefs. Money spent to get a child into a top private school to maximize the chance of success relative to others, for example, comes at the expense of money that could have been spent inculcating trust-producing moral beliefs that benefit society. One parent can reduce investment in the latter to improve his own child's prospects with no chance of harming the high-trust society. But when all parents do this, the high-trust society is undermined and therefore the future welfare of everyone's children is reduced.

A closely related problem is that even those who value investing heavily in morality don't distinguish between social human capital in the form of prosocial tastes and duty-based moral restraint. All else the same, nicer people are better for society. But with economic activity, we don't need people to be nice to get them to do what is best for society because transactions that promote the common good are mutually beneficial. To get the most out of cooperation, however, we do need people to be trustworthy and to have trust in the system.

The erosion of social human capital is likely feeding on itself. Children are not good at teaching what is required to rise above thinking and acting like a child. For this reason most children who are raised by children will, in some ways, remain children forever. For reasons Daniel Patrick Moynihan laid out in his infamous 1965 report, this is a road to disaster.[1] As he also predicted, this is no longer just a "breakdown of the black family" problem.

Children start life being completely self-centered because there is no other possible way for them to be. A hallmark of adulthood is, in contrast, an increasing preoccupation with the lives and welfare of others. Think about the most adult people you know. Is it not true that they spend a great deal of time thinking about others? Think about the most immature people you know. Is it not true that they spend a great deal of time thinking about themselves? And when they do think about others, is it not often just to figure out how to get what they want from them?

I submit that what is happening in the West is nothing less than widespread and accelerating infantilization. It is accelerating because each generation has fewer genuine adults to raise the next. We are increasingly a people who think more about what our family, friends, communities, and country can do for us rather than what we can do for them. We focus on the petty and the small, and in so doing we are becoming petty and small. I shall now offer three speculations for why this is happening.

The Wages of Success

The West shows signs of its success sowing the seeds of its demise along the lines laid out in chapter 7. Success weakens incentives for adequate investment into trust-producing moral beliefs. Success also strengthens incentives for promulgating deleterious moral beliefs that appeal to our small-group moral intuitions. So success leads to having too little of what is needed to sustain the high-trust society and too much of that which undermines it.

In countries like the United States there was, for a time, the best of both worlds. There were prevailing moral beliefs that stressed duty-based moral restraint over moral advocacy. At the same time the insufficient investment problem was overcome to some extent through strong incentives for human capital investment for the benefit of the family. Until about a century ago, children were so important for supporting the family that they were heavily invested in to become good workers at a very young age.

Over this period capitalism became increasingly viewed as morally respectable, so market competition became morally respectable. Families were therefore exposed to the competitive pressures of free market pricing. This put even more pressure on parents to make their children good workers, which increased the level of social human capital investment. But as I explained in chapter 8, over the course of the 20th century technological improvements have made children ever poorer inputs to production. At the same time, the return to the family from investing in trust producing culture has fallen as the need for formal schooling has increased. So mechanisms that helped overcome the insufficient investment problem weakened dramatically over the course of the 20th century.

Multiculturalism

Humans thrive when honest competition is applied to a diversity of ideas. The greater the diversity of ideas and the more vigorous is competition over them, the faster superior ideas will be replicated and inferior ones will be discarded. So societies that have a variety of ethnic groups, races, religions, ways of life, and ways of thinking are more vibrant, competitive, and successful than insular societies.

But what if a particular culture does not believe in the value of diversity as an end in itself or does not care about the social benefits of having competing ideas? What if that culture views all other cultures as evil? What if that culture thinks that allowing honest and open competition between diverse ideas is likely to corrupt their children?

This, in a nutshell, is the problem with multiculturalism. As a stand-alone ideal without qualification, it is internally inconsistent. If having respect for all cultures requires welcoming those that will not return the favor, then the result is quite the opposite of the original intention. A society may very well end up being less tolerant than it was when it started taking tolerance seriously. For this reason there is nothing hypocritical about endorsing cultural diversity while disapproving of those cultures that do not.

Multiculturalism presents an additional challenge to democracies. Mancur Olson explained how the separation of people into special interest groups can undermine the democratic process. As the stakes rise from using the democratic process as a political spoils system, suspicion and cynicism rise, because this system creates winners and losers, thereby stoking tribalism. Such tribalism will naturally be stronger if the motivation for the special interest group is ethnic, racial, or religious identity.

For the reasons laid out in chapter 7, tribalism destabilizes democracy. It leads to more redistribution from one group to another and therefore leads to more anger and suspicion between groups. As the stakes of elections grow, it increases the likelihood of cheating. This undermines faith in the democratic process, ultimately undermining trust in the system.

Tribalism is devastating to a free market democracy because it is antithetical to large-group trust and the high-trust society. It bottles up highly trust-dependent transactions into groups small enough to sustain trust through our innate moral intuitions. This dramatically reduces a society's ability to produce the general prosperity required for mass flourishing.

So having diverse cultures that can provide diverse perspectives to inform scientific inquiry, business practices, political debate, and policy design is one thing. Having diverse cultures that create multiple nodes of political identity that can coalesce into special interest groups that seek to promote their welfare at the expense of the common good is quite another. The former can invigorate a free market democracy, while the latter can destroy it.

Tribalism also erodes our basic decency. Our natural sense of empathy is a bulwark against evil. Tribalism is a way of overcoming our sense of empathy so we can do harsh things to our enemies. When our hunter-gatherer ancestors went on raids to kill members of other bands, doing so was easier if they viewed those to be killed as *them*. When tribalism is stoked, empathy is suppressed. Even if unintended, this can allow indecency to emerge. Just consider national politics in the United States. As it becomes more tribal, does it not also become more indecent?

When tribalism undermines empathy, individualism also suffers. When we think of other people as unique individuals, our sense of empathy is more acute. This is true even if we don't know the individuals personally because our capacity for empathy induces us to try to imagine them as unique individuals rather than as identical silhouettes.

When we think of people as identical silhouettes, it is easier to think of *them* as homogeneous elements of a different set from *us*. This makes it easier for a group to draw a sharp contrast between it and other groups. But that also produces pressure for conformity in one's own group. Tribalism therefore does more than dehumanize those in other groups. It also suppresses individualism within our own group. Conversely, individualism impedes such attempts at objectification. Individualism is therefore something we should take seriously. It is not a mere euphemism for selfishness.

Societies that wish to foster mass flourishing give up too much when they give up on cultural diversity. But those concerned about the risks of multiculturalism should not be dismissed as mere cultural chauvinists. I submit that if one understands how trust-producing culture produces high-trust societies and mass flourishing, one is in a better position to promulgate ideological beliefs that create common ground across cultural groups.

Finding such common ground is not a fanciful proposition. For many years the number of new immigrants coming to America was extraordinary. Most wanted a better life but were still proud of their heritage and planned to keep up their religious and cultural practices. But most also strapped on new ideological beliefs about the virtues of individualism, freedom, separation of church and state, and the rule of law.

For the most part, these ideas neither endorsed nor conflicted with the existing beliefs of most immigrants because they operated at a different level of generality.[2] This created an overarching culture that all Americans shared, and the cultures immigrants brought with them became, effectively, subcultures that they continued to cherish. At the same time, those from other cultures also valued the ability to experience yet another culture different from their own.

Those who embrace multiculturalism without insisting on some ground rules do not take culture seriously. If culture were no more than innocuous practices involving the dances we dance, the foods we eat, and the holidays we celebrate, then concern over the fact that others have a different culture would be mere chauvinism.

But suppose one believes that only culture can adequately convey the moral beliefs required to sustain a thriving free market democracy. Suppose that one also believes that one's home culture has done reasonably well conveying those beliefs. In that case, one would be foolish not to consider whether immigrants bring with them an eagerness to add the prevailing culture of their new home to their own culture or an eagerness to overturn the culture of their new home.

Freedom

A prevailing ethic of duty-based moral restraint is not merely consistent with freedom. It is hard to imagine that freedom can exist for human beings in any other way. Duty-based moral restraint does not tell people what to do, it only tells what them what not to do. This leaves the set of all other actions—both existing and those yet to be discovered—to the discretion and judgment of the individual. Nothing else cuts closer to the heart of practical freedom.

In the West we are seeing an escalation of the police state in response to growing anger from those who feel disenfranchised. I contend that much of this is the result of societies in the West taking their success for granted, which has led them to fail to invest adequately in trust-producing culture. This has necessitated an increasing reliance on government institutions to achieve what used to be achieved by private individuals, families, and organizations through culture. The result has been an erosion of freedom with far-reaching results.

Culture can convey ideological beliefs that keep democracy from destroying itself by making voters unwilling to allow the democratic process to be used to engage in redistributive and regulatory favoritism. But trust-producing culture also protects freedom as a state of mind. As long as we are not completely alone, we will not endorse absolute freedom. If other people are free to do whatever they want, that could include making us very miserable. So all adults understand that any workable conception of freedom must abide by the adage: *Your freedom to swing your arms ends at my nose.*

For freedom to be meaningful, then, we have to account for how we will limit it without killing it. Institutions limit freedom so we don't make each other miserable through incentives to keep people from doing what they would otherwise do. Trust-producing culture takes an entirely different approach. Trust-producing culture redacts the set of actions through moral tastes. This makes people not want to do what society does not want them to do. Accordingly, society gets the behavior it wants not by forcing people to do or to not do things, but by instantiating values that incline them to want to do or not do what is best for society.

This keeps people from doing that which bothers others in a way that does not reduce their sense of freedom. It produces social harmony not through punishments and rewards but through character. Character provides a flexible basis for moral restraint that does not fail to function in novel situations that existing patterns and institutions have never encountered.

The distinction between civilized behavior arising from incentives and civilized behavior arising from moral character is epitomized by the mythical stereotype of the individualistic cowboy. He doesn't claim to know all the laws and makes no pretense of caring about the welfare of strangers. Yet he is trusted by all because he always keeps his word even among people he has never met before and knows he will never see again.

He doesn't need punishments and rewards to be eschew opportunism. His distaste for opportunism is about the kind of man he believes himself to be. He doesn't lie because he is not a liar. He doesn't steal because he is not a thief. No matter where he rides, no matter who he comes across, and no matter what the circumstance of the moment are, the one thing that doesn't change in the story is who he is. He possesses virtue character in the finest sense of Aristotle, and he lives in our minds as a myth in idealized form in the finest sense of Plato.

The mythical cowboy may be proud of who he is, but he cannot take credit for it. He correctly credits his ma and pa for anything that might be good about him. He is the product of a cultural foundation of individualism derived from emphasis on character that is a product of years of hard work and investment by his parents, teachers, and other adults. This is not the caricature of individualism as selfishness, for if one is both selfish and powerful, one exploits others when he can, and our mythical cowboy never does. He understands that individualism is not a license to harm others any more than freedom is a license to do whatever one wants.

I submit that those who live in free market democracies value freedom as much as a state of mind as they do as a political condition. It is important to feel free and to think in ways that only free persons do. When culture imprints a great deal of behavior through practices, this has the effect of crowding out freedom of action and freedom of mind. Even creativity is suppressed.

The more a society invests into the inculcation of duty-based moral restraint, the less the society will have to rely on formal institutions and government power to maintain enough order so people will not feel compelled to surrender freedom in return for order. Such self-regulation requires massive intergenerational investment in culture. The benefits are realized by the next generation, not the one whose sacrifices made the benefits possible. We correctly credit our patriots with preserving our freedom, but without this sacrifice from one generation to the next there is little freedom for patriots to fight for.

Final Thoughts

So what should we do? Trust-producing culture needs both trust-producing moral beliefs and a very high level of investment into their inculcation. But it is ultimately the content of moral beliefs that matters most because moral beliefs can affect the level of investment.

Changing prevailing beliefs is hard, but we have done it before. Recall that the environmental movement was basically nonexistent in 1960. But by 1975 the National Environmental Protection Act, the Coastal Zone Management Act, the Endangered Species Act, and the National Wild and Scenic Rivers Act were enacted into law and the Environmental Protection Agency was created. The real change, the lasting change, was the effect that environmental activists had on our culture.

These changes were not forced upon voters by government. Instead, voters forced the government to get serious about stopping the harm being done to the environment. Activists changed our beliefs so thoroughly that the vast majority of people in the United States today would be regarded as extreme environmentalists by the average person in 1960. People were persuaded about the need to work for a cleaner environment, and politicians of both parties figured out quickly that one way to get elected was to support policies to make that happen. Few individuals thought their efforts would tip the balance, but that didn't matter. Voters came to believe that it was their moral duty to press for such change.

An even more powerful example was the civil rights movement. The genius of Dr. Martin Luther King was to put the injustice of racism, much of which was institutionalized through the power of government, right before the nose of ordinary voters. He was careful not to give voters any excuse for dismissing what they saw by urging his followers to be nonviolent. Over time the truth could no longer be denied or rationalized.

Things then started changing for the better, but it was not by enlisting government power to make the majority do what they didn't want to do. It was *the majority* of voters who forced federal, state, and local governments to stop using their power to perpetuate injustice. Few individuals thought their individual actions would tip the balance, but that didn't matter. Dr. King's approach bet on the flexibility and power of culture. As he had hoped, over time the majority of voters came to believe that it was their moral duty to press for such change.

Contrary to what many models in mainstream economics suggest, people sometimes act to promote the common good even if they know their individual actions change nothing. They simply want to do the right thing. This does not mean they are irrational; it means that most models in economics fail to adequately model rational behavior. In any case, many people already have moral beliefs that comport with morality being a matter of duty.[3] This suggests that if moral activists and teachers turn to helping people understand how utterly dependent the high-trust society is on a prevailing ethic of duty-based moral restraint, citizens may come to conclude that it is their moral duty to do their part by raising their children to abide by that ethic.

***

The story of the rise of human civilization is largely a story of how a small-group species was able to overcome its small-group limitations. But since our genes don't adapt as fast as culture and institutions do, we remain largely a small-group species. Our success is therefore like a jet airliner flying overhead in a moment-by-moment struggle with gravity that never stops pulling it to the ground. This is why countless stories have been devoted to the theme of heroic individuals who do not put self ahead of the common good.

By making the high-trust society possible, trust-producing culture can lift us far beyond what our ancestors, just a few centuries ago, thought possible. But if, instead, culture conveys moral beliefs that indulge our small-group moral intuitions, it produces the antithesis of large-group cooperation—it produces tribalism. Tribalism is to us what gravity is to a jet airliner. It never stops pulling down on the high-trust society. Unfortunately, evidence that tribalism is alive and well is all around us.

As a restless species that endeavors to achieve much, overcoming tribalism has been our greatest achievement. But overcoming tribalism is a job that is never finished. The end of history will never arrive for free market democracies, because their continued success increasingly opens the door to failure.[4] The democracy that high-trust societies make possible gives tribalism an opening to turn back the clock of human societal development through political favoritism that pits some of us against the rest of us, in the process making it harder for there to be an "us."

One cannot help but feel that there is something unsettling about effectuating social control through moral tastes that are better described as having been absorbed by young children than as having been chosen by adults. It is, frankly, a kind of mind control. Anyone raised in a free society naturally worries that this undermines individualism.

But what is the alternative?

If our children grow up in a moral vacuum, most will adopt beliefs that come most naturally to them, which are moral beliefs that comport with their innate small-group moral intuitions. In such a society, adults will act with the insecurity, narcissism, self-righteous indignation, and need for continuous social approval of a middle school student. Such adults can neither build nor sustain high-trust societies.

Ultimately the adults of any given generation must decide what they will teach their children. As with any hard decision, it is best to start with facts. Here are a few. Children start out life very impressionable. What they learn earliest is better described as being absorbed than being chosen. What they learn earliest also frames how they think about everything they learn later, including how it fits into their continuously evolving theory of right and wrong and how the world works.

If we truly care about future generations, then we have to ask ourselves what we must teach our children if they are to grow up to become the kind of adults who can sustain the kind of society they will want to live in. This requires teaching moral beliefs that work in light of the big picture and the long run even though our genes drive us to focus on the here and now. This requires inculcating children with a civic sense of duty-based moral restraint and a belief that moral advocacy is a private matter, and then later telling them exactly what we did and why we did it, urging them to do the same thing for their own children.

Because thriving free market democracies are wellsprings of creativity and juggernauts of cooperation, they are our best hope for ensuring that each future generation leaves a better society for the next. Trust-producing culture is our best hope for sustaining the high-trust society that makes such societies possible, so leaving what our children learn to chance is foolish. If we don't teach our children the kind of moral beliefs that put moral restraint first, making them trustworthy individuals who can sustain a high-trust society, then others, or their small-group genes, will teach them something else.

Notes

1. Daniel Patrick Moynihan (1965), *The Negro Family: The Case for National Action*.

2. There are religions that do not approve of the separation of church and state. In societies whose governments comport with such religions, we see neither cultural diversity nor its benefits.

3. See again Bryan Caplan's (2007) *The Myth of the Rational Voter* for a discussion of evidence that indicates that most people try to vote what their conscience dictates. This comports with thinking about moral behavior in terms of moral duty.

4. The end of history is a reference to a famous claim made by Francis Fukuyama (1992) in his book *The End of History and the Last Man*.

Bibliography

Acemoglu, Daron, and James A. Robinson. 2012. *Why Nations Fail*. New York: Crown Publishing.

Adams, John, and Abigail Adams. 2003. *The Letters of John and Abigail Adams*. London: Penguin.

Ahn, T. K., and Elinor Ostrom, eds. 2003. *Critical Studies in Economic Institutions: Foundations of Social Capital*. Cheltenham, UK: Edward Elgar.

Alesina, Alberto. 2013. "Political Economy." *NBER Reporter*, July.

Alesina, Alberto, and Paola Guiliano. 2015. "Culture and Institutions." *Journal of Economic Literature* 53(4): 898–944.

Algan, Yann, and Pierre Cahuc. 2010. "Inherited Trust and Growth." *American Economic Review* 100(5): 2060–2092.

Axelrod, Robert. 1984. *The Evolution of Cooperation*. New York: Basic Books.

Baker, G., Robert Gibbons, and K. J. Murphy. 2002. "Relational Contracts and the Theory of the Firm." *Quarterly Journal of Economics* 117(1): 39–84.

Becker, Gary. 1964. *Human Capital*. Chicago: University of Chicago Press.

Bisin, Alberto, and Thierry Verdier. 2017. "On the Joint Evolution of Culture and Institutions." NBER Working Paper No. 23375, April.

Bodoh-Creed, Aaron L. 2017. "Endogenous Institutional Selection, Building Trust, and Economic Growth." Mimeo, University of California-Berkeley, Haas School of Business, September.

Boehm, Christopher. 2012. *Moral Origins: The Evolution of Virtue, Altruism, and Shame*. New York: Basic Books.

Bowles, Samuel, and Herbert Gintis. 2011. *A Cooperative Species*. Princeton, NJ: Princeton University Press.

Boyd, Robert, and Peter J. Richerson. 1985. *Culture and the Evolutionary Process*. Chicago: University of Chicago Press.

Brooks, David. 2015. *The Road to Character*. New York: Random House.

Brownworth, Lars. 2014. *The Sea Wolves: A History of the Vikings*. London: United Kingdom: Crux Publishing.

Buchanan, James M. 1987. "Budgetary Bias in Post-Keynesian Politics: The Erosion and Potential Replacement of Fiscal Norms." In *Deficits*, edited by James M. Buchanan, Charles K. Rowley, and Robert D. Tollison. New York: Blackwell, 180–198.

Caplan, Bryan. 2007. *The Myth of the Rational Voter: Why Democracies Choose Bad Policies*. Princeton, NJ: Princeton University Press.

Churchill, Winston. 1998. "Speech in the House of Commons." 11 November 1947. In *Churchill Speaks: Collected Speeches in Peace and War, 1897–1963*. New York: Barnes & Noble.

Coase, Ronald H. 1937. "The Nature of the Firm." *Economica* 16(4): 386–405.

———. 1960. "The Problem of Social Cost." *Journal of Law and Economics* 3 (October): 1–44.

Covey, Steven M. R. 2006. *The Speed of Trust: The One Thing That Changes Everything*. New York: Free Press.

Coward, F., and Robin I. M. Dunbar. 2014. "Communities on the Edge of Civilisation." In *Lucy to Language: The Benchmark Papers*, edited by Robin I. M. Dunbar, Clive Gamble, and J. A. J. Gowlett. Oxford: Oxford University Press, 380–405.

Darwin, Charles. 1871. *Descent of Man, and Selection in Relation to Sex*. London: John Murray.

Dawkins, Richard. 1976. *The Selfish Gene*. New York: Oxford University Press.

de Soto, Hernando. 2000. *The Mystery of Capital: Why Capitalism Triumphs in the West and Fails Everywhere Else*. New York: Basic Books.

Demsetz, Harold. 1997. "The Firm of Theory: Its Definition and Existence." In *The Economics of the Business Firm: Seven Critical Commentaries*. Cambridge: Cambridge University Press, 1–14.

Diamond, Jared. 1987. "The Worst Mistake in the History of the Human Race." *Discover Magazine*, May, 64–66.

Dunbar, Robin I. M. 2016. *Human Evolution*. New York: Oxford University Press.

Durlauf, Steven N., and Marcel Fafchamps. 2006. "Social Capital." In *Handbook of Economic Growth*, Vol. 1, edited by Philippe Aghion and Steven N. Durlauf. Amsterdam: North Holland, 1639–1699.

Elster, Jon. 1989. *Nuts and Bolts for the Social Sciences.* Cambridge: Cambridge University Press.

Ferguson, Niall. 2008. *The Ascent of Money: A Financial History of the World*. New York: Penguin.

———. 2013. *The Great Degeneration: How Institutions Decay and Economies Die.* New York: Penguin.

Fournier, Ron, and Sophie Quinton. 2012. "How Americans Lost Trust in Our Greatest Institutions." *The Atlantic*, 20 April.

Frank, Robert H. 1988. *Passions within Reason: The Strategic Role of the Emotions.* New York: Norton.

———. 1999. *Luxury Fever.* New York: Free Press.

Friedman, Milton. 1981. *Capitalism and Freedom.* Chicago: University of Chicago Press.

Fukuyama, Francis. 1992. *The End of History and the Last Man.* New York: Free Press.

———. 1995. *Trust: The social Virtues And the Creation of Prosperity.* New York: Free Press.

Gintis, Herbert. 2011. "Gene-Culture Coevolution and the Nature of Human Sociality." *Philosophical Transactions of the Royal Society* 366: 878–888.

Gladwell, Malcolm. 2000. *The Tipping Point: How Little Things Make a Big Difference.* Boston: Little, Brown.

Glaeser, Edward L., Laibson, David, and Bruce Sacerdote. 2002. "An Economic Approach to Social Capital." *Economic Journal* 112(483): F437–F458.

Gneezy, Uri. 2005. "Deception: The Role of Consequences." *American Economic Review* 95(1): 384–394.

Gorodnichenko, Yuriy, and Gerard Roland. 2010. "Culture, Institutions, and the Wealth of Nations." NBER Working Paper No. 16368, September.

———. 2011. "Which Dimensions of Culture Matter for Long-Run Growth?" *American Economic Review* 101(3): 492–498.

Granovetter, Mark. 1978. "Threshold Models of Collective Behavior." *American Journal of Sociology* 83(6): 1420–1443.

Greif, Avner. 1993. "Contract Enforceability and Economic Institutions in Early Trade: The Maghribi Trader's Coalition." *American Economic Review* 83(3): 525–548.

———. 2006. *Institutions and the Path to the Modern Economy: Lessons from Medieval Trade*. New York: Cambridge University Press.

Guiso, Sapienza, and Luigi Zingales. 2008. "Social Capital as Good Culture." *Journal of the European Economic Association* 6(2–3): 295–320.

Haidt, Jonathan. 2012. *The Righteous Mind: Why Good People Are Divided by Politics and Religion*. New York: Pantheon.

Hardin, Garrett. 1968. "The Tragedy of the Commons." *Science* 162(3859): 1243–1248.

Hardin, Russell. 2002. *Trust and Trustworthiness*. New York: Russell Sage Foundation.

Harrison, Lawrence E., and Samuel P. Huntington, eds. 2000. *Culture Matters: How Values Shape Human Progress*. New York: Basic Books.

Hayek, F. A. 1945. "The Use of Knowledge in Society." *American Economic Review* 35(4): 519–530.

———. 1988. *The Fatal Conceit: The Errors of Socialism*. Chicago: University of Chicago Press.

Hebb, Donald. 1949. *The Organization of Behavior*. New York: Wiley & Sons.

Heinlein, Robert A. 1987. *To Sail beyond the Sunset*. New York: Putnam.

Henrich, Joseph. 2016. *The Secret of Our Success: How Culture Is Driving Human Evolution, Domesticating Our Species, and Making Us Smarter*. Princeton, NJ: Princeton University Press.

Henrich, Natalie, and Joseph Henrich. 2007. *Why Humans Cooperate: A Cultural and Evolutionary Explanation*. New York: Oxford University Press.

Holcombe, Randall G. 2002. *From Liberty to Democracy: The Transformation of American Government*. Ann Arbor: University of Michigan Press.

Jones, Eric L. 2006. *Cultures Merging: A Historical and Economic Critique of Culture*. Princeton, NJ: Princeton University Press.

Knack, Stephen, and Philip Keefer. 1997. "Does Social Capital Have an Economic Payoff? A Cross-Country Investigation." *Quarterly Journal of Economics* 112(4): 1251–1288.

Knack, Stephen, and Paul J. Zak. 2001. "Trust and Growth." *Economic Journal* 111(470): 295–321.

La Macchia, Stephen T., Winnifred R. Louis, Matthew J. Hornsey, and Geoffrey J. Leonardelli. 2016. "In Small We Trust: Lay Theories about Small and Large Groups." *Personality and Social Psychology Bulletin* 42(10): 1321–1334.

Landes, David. 2000. "Culture Makes Almost All the Difference." In *Culture Matters: How Values Shape Human Progress*, edited by Lawrence E. Harrison and Samuel P. Huntington. New York: Basic Books, 2–13.

Lawrence, D. H. (1931) 1996. *Apocalypse*. London: Penguin.

Levi, Margaret. 1998. "A State of Trust." In *Trust and Governance*, edited by Margaret Levi and Valerie Braithwaite. New York: Russell Sage, 77–101.

Lloyd, William Forster. 1833. *Two Lectures on the Checks to Population*. Self-published.

Lowel, Siegrid, and W. Singer. 1992. "Selection of Intrinsic Horizontal Connections in the Visual Cortex by Correlated Neuronal Activity." *Science* 255(5041): 209–212.

Lowes, Sara, Nathan Nunn, James A. Robinson, and Jonathan Weigel. 2015. "The Evolution of Culture and Institutions: Evidence from the Kuba Kingdom." NBER Working Paper No. 21798, December.

Luttmer, Erzo F. P., and Monica Singhal. 2011. "Culture, Context, and the Taste for Redistribution." *American Economic Journal: Economic Policy* 3: 157–179.

Macaulay, Stewart. 1963. "Non-contractual Relations in Business." *American Sociological Review* 28(1): 55–70.

Macneil, Ian Roderick. 1978. "Contracts: Adjustments of long-Term Economic Relations under Classical, Neoclassical, and Relational Contract Law." *Northwestern University Law Review* 72(6): 854–906.

Mann, Thomas E., and Norman J. Ornstein. 2012. *It's Even Worse Than it Looks: How the American Constitutional System Collided with the New Politics of Extremism*. New York: Basic Books.

Marcus, Gary. 2004. *The Birth of the Mind*. New York: Basic Books.

McCloskey, Deirdre N. 2006. *The Bourgeois Virtues: Ethics for an Age of Commerce*. Chicago: University of Chicago Press.

———. 2010. *Bourgeois Dignity: Why Economics Can't Explain the Modern World*. Chicago: University of Chicago Press.

———. 2014. *Bourgeois Equality: How Ideas, Not Capital or Institutions, Enriched the World*. Chicago: University of Chicago Press.

Moynihan, Daniel Patrick. 1965. *The Negro Family: The Case for National Action* Washington, DC: Office of Policy Planning and Research, US Department of Labor.

North, Douglass C. 2005. *Understanding the Process of Change*. Princeton, NJ: Princeton University Press.

Olson, Mancur. 1965. *The Logic of Collective Action: Public Goods and the Theory of Groups*. Cambridge, MA: Harvard University Press.

―――. 1982. *The Rise and Decline of Nations: Economic Growth, Stagnation, and Social Rigidities*. New Haven: Yale University Press.

―――. 1993. "Dictatorship, Democracy, and Development." *American Political Science Review* 87(3): 567–576.

Ortiz-Ospina, Esteban, and Max Roser. 2017. "Trust." Retrieved from https://ourworldindata.org/trust.

Ostrom, Elinor. 1990. *Governing the Commons: The Evolution of Institutions for Collective Action*. Cambridge: Cambridge University Press.

―――. 2003. "Toward a Behavioral Theory Linking Trust, Reciprocity, and Reputation." In *Trust and Reciprocity: Interdisciplinary Lessons from Experimental Research*, edited by Elinor Ostrom and James Walker. New York: Russell Sage Foundation, 19–79.

Otteson, James R. 2002. *Adam Smith's Marketplace of Life*. Cambridge: Cambridge University Press.

Phelps, Edmund. 2013. *Mass Flourishing: How Grassroots Innovation Created Jobs, Challenge, and Change*. Princeton, NJ: Princeton University Press.

Pipes, Richard. 1999. *Property and Freedom*. New York: Alfred Knopf.

Regulatory Policy Institute. 2009. *Trust in the System: Restoring Trust in Our System of Government and Regulation*. Oxford: Regulatory Policy Institute.

Richerson, Peter J., and Robert Boyd. 2005. *Not by Genes Alone*. Chicago: University of Chicago Press.

Richerson, Peter J., Robert Boyd, and Joseph Henrich. 2010. "Gene-Culture Coevolution in the Age of Genomics." *Proceedings of the National Academy of Sciences* 107, supplement 2, 8985–8992.

Ridley, Matt. 1997. *The Origins of Virtue: Human Instincts and the Evolution of Cooperation*. New York: Viking Penguin.

Roberts, Russell. 1995. "If You're Paying, I'll Have Top Sirloin." *Wall Street Journal*, 18 May.

Romer, Paul M. 1994. "The Origins of Endogenous Growth." *Journal of Economic Perspectives* 8(1): 3–22.

Root, Hilton L. 2006. *Capital and Collusion: Political Logic of Global Economic Development*. Princeton, NJ: Princeton University Press.

―――. 2008. *Alliance Curse: How the U.S. Lost the Third World*. Washington, DC: Brookings Institution Press.

Rose, David C. 2000. "Teams, Firms, and the Evolution of Profit Seeking Behavior." *Journal of Bioeconomics* 2(1): 25–39.

———. 2002. "Marginal Productivity Analysis in Teams." *Journal of Economic Behavior and Organization* 48(4): 355–363.

———. 2011. *The Moral Foundation of Economic Behavior.* New York: Oxford University Press.

———. 2016. "Virtues as Social Capital." In *Economics and the Virtues,* edited by Mark D. White and Jennifer Baker. New York: Oxford University Press, 202–216.

Sachs, Jeffrey. 2005. *The End of Poverty: Economic Possibilities for Our Time.* New York: Penguin Books.

Schelling, Thomas C. 1978. *Micromotives and Macrobehavior.* New York: Norton.

Smith, Adam. (1759) 1982. *The Theory of Moral Sentiments.* Edited by D. D. Raphael and A. L. Macfie. Indianapolis: Liberty Fund Press.

———. (1776) 1981. *An Inquiry into the Nature and Causes of the Wealth of Nations.* Edited by R. H. Campbell and A. S. Skinner, Indianapolis: Liberty Fund Press.

Smith, John Maynard. 1982. *Evolution and the Theory of Games.* Cambridge: Cambridge University Press.

Sobel, Joel. 2002. "Can We Trust Social Capital?" *Journal of Economic Literature* 40(1): 139–154.

Solow, Robert M. 1956. "A Contribution to the Theory of Economic Growth." *Quarterly Journal of Economics* 70(1): 65–94.

Stigler, Stigler. 1971. "The Theory of Economic Regulation." *Bell Journal of Economics and Management Science* 3: 3–18.

Swift, Art. 2016. "Americans' Trust in Mass Media Sinks to New Low." *Politics,* 14 September, Gallup. Retrieved from http://news.gallup.com/poll/195542/americans-trust-mass-media-sinks-new-low.aspx.

Tabellini, Guido. 2010. "Culture and Institutions: Economic Development in the Regions of Europe." *Journal of the European Economic Association* 8(4): 677–716.

Uslaner, Eric M. 2002. *The Moral Foundations of Trust.* Cambridge: Cambridge University Press.

Wade, Lizzie. 2015. "Birth of the Moralizing Gods." *Science* 349(6251): 919–922.

Walton, Gary M., and Hugh Rockoff. 2014. *History of the American Economy.* 12th ed. Mason, OH: Southwestern Publishing.

Weatherford, J. McIver. 1988. *Indian Givers: How the Indians of the Americas Transformed the World.* New York: Fawcett Columbine.

Wilson, David Sloan. 2002. *Darwin's Cathedral: Evolution, Religion, and the Nature of Society*. Chicago: University of Chicago Press.

Yamagishi, Toshio. 2000. *Trust*. Tokyo: Springer.

Index

Figures are indicated by an italic *f* following the page number.

Printed in the USA/Agawam, MA
November 26, 2021

785163.023